# MUSIC LICENSING FOR FILMS
## WHAT A PRODUCER SHOULD KNOW
### WRITTEN BY PAULO LEITE

Title: "MUSIC LICENSING FOR FILMS: WHAT A PRODUCER SHOULD KNOW"
Author: PAULO LEITE
Text: © 2017 PAULO LEITE
All photos and images © 2017 LAULO LEITE
All Rights Reserved.
FIRST EDITION
ISBN: 9781973281993
Independently Published.
For any comments, suggestions, questions regarding this book
or the author, please send us an email to: badbehavior@badbehavior.pt
If you want to quote this book, a written permission can easily be obtained from
the author.
www.BadBehavior.pt
https://BadBehavior.wordpress.com/

# CONTENTS

PAULO LEITE

## ABOUT THE AUTHOR

PAULO LEITE (writer/producer) was born in Recife, Brazil, and has over 20 years of professional experience. He has worked in Production roles in Film, TV, Commercials and Fashion. Paulo also has experience in Development, having helped many international producers with their projects, either as a writer, consultant, mentor or simply as a friend. Paulo teaches film production at Lisbon's Film School and is a life-long, hardcore horror fan with a massive book, DVD and VHS collection to prove it. An avid music collector, Paulo has over 10.000 CDs and vinyl records. He is on Facebook, Linkedin and Twitter. He also attends all the main film festivals and markets in Europe, North and Latin America and is frequently hired as a lecturer/speaker on themes like film development, story editing, screenwriting, horror films, film marketing and other engaging subjects. He holds degrees in Film Production, Screenwriting and Communication Sciences.

PAULO LEITE

To Wanessa. To Michael.

To the awesome horror community worldwide. Just like you, I love horror films and I want to help you make your own films.

To all my friends who have helped and inspired me along the way.

## INTRODUCTION

This book was designed as a quick tool for young producers who want to make a great horror film (or any film you want to make, really, since the stuff we are covering here applies to any film from any genre) and need to know the basics about how to get music for their films.

Music is a big part of any film. Just think about the shower scene in PSYCHO (1960) without Bernard Herrmann's strings playing violently as Janet Leigh meets her fate. Or think about Dan O'Bannon's brilliant use of Roky Erickson's "Burn the Flames" when Frank commits suicide in THE RETURN OF THE LIVING DEAD (1985).

Better yet: think about the transformation scene in the classic AN AMERICAN WEREWOLF IN LONDON (1981). Would Rick Baker's amazing make-up wizardry feel the same in silence without Sam Cooke's version of "Blue Moon" playing in the background? Would it feel the same with some free music taken from Youtube? Of course not.

What's new with this edition?

Well, I added a few images to make it clearer how things work, and rewrote some passages for more accuracy. I also added some images explaining the flow of royalties, fees and licenses that I hope will be very helpful to anyone who wants to understand how the music industry works. I also added Madonna's very complex RAY OF LIGHT case study – a fascinating example of the many layers a song can have and more questions on the Q&A section.

A BIG THANK YOU to my dear friend KENNY OCHOA from QUIVER for the peer-reviewing. Another BIG THANK YOU to those who took some time to read, help me improve the content and gave me all the great feedback.

Enjoy your book!
Paulo Leite

# 1 – THE BASICS: WHAT'S AT STAKE HERE?

Music rights are a nightmare to young producers. They're expensive, complex and they do have an impact on the success of your film. It's easy to make mistakes here; waste time and blow up your budget.

So, let's start.

There are basically two types of music in a film.

DIEGETIC MUSIC (comes from the narrative and can be listened by the characters – like when a character turns on the radio while driving).

NON-DIEGETIC MUSIC (comes from outside the story and can only be heard by the audience – like the frenetic strings we hear when the monster is approaching and the characters are desperately trying to escape).

From that, there are several questions a young producer can ask: how do I get the music? Who do I ask for it? What should I ask? What do I need? What is the fair price? What am I paying for? What are my obligations? What can I do or cannot do with music?

Music has the power to do a lot of things for a film. It can create and enhance emotions you want the audience to feel. Sometimes the emotion is already on the screen without the music, but then you add the music and it simply takes that emotion to a whole different level. Beyond that, music can also synchronize the emotions felt by characters and audiences. A great score can mark the exact time when the audience will feel what the character is feeling. Music can also capture a certain spirit that is needed for a scene. Whether it is the coronation of a king or a day in high-school in the summer of 1977, music can instantly transport the audience there with the efficacy image alone cannot have. Music can also prolong and manage expectations in the viewer. The murderer is observing the victim. Music helps us sustain the moment giving us the perception that time has distended. Music is also a great marketing tool. The trailer of THE ICE AGE 3: DAWN OF THE DINOSAURS (2009) brilliantly uses "You'll Never Find Another Love Like Mine" (Gamble/Huff) by Lou Rawls, making us laugh at the silly seduction games between two animated characters.

There is also a recognizability quality that certain songs bring into a film. It's hard to remember two or three scenes from Adrian Lyne's 9 ½ WEEKS (1986), but there is one scene everybody can remember and it's, to a large extent, due to the use of Joe Cocker's awesome cover of a Randy Newman song. And of course, music can just be a fun element that can comment on the film itself. Filmmakers as different as Mel Brooks and Quentin Tarantino perfectly use the reflexive element of music.

The first thing you should understand is the difference between all the entities and things involved in making a song. There are dozens, of course, but when it comes to music in films, the following two are the most important:

THE SONG ITSELF (musical notes in a specific order and the lyrics that come with it) that belongs to its composers.

THE MASTER RECORDING (of that song) that belongs to whoever paid for it and made it happen (sometimes the artist, sometimes the record label that has the artist under contract).

*Lesson number one: choose your music carefully. It is as important as your characters. Music actually is another character! Maybe not a physical one, but a more pervasive, spiritual one.*

Now, before we go any further, let's discuss two things that sometimes leave people puzzled: the difference between clearing a song (or getting a clearance for a song) and licensing a song.

The clearance happens early on. Sometimes you are thinking about a song because you would like to write a scene around it or because you are not sure you want to convince your producer to use it. Sometimes you'll find websites that say "pre-cleared" songs. Well, clearance is when you get a confirmation that the song you want is available for licensing, the conditions under which it can be licensed, and the costs involved. If you are a composer/musician, you can pre-clear all of your songs. If you are a filmmaker, you can create a list of songs you have cleared (so you can budget more accurately).

The licensing will take place later, when you decide to use the song and you are ready to meet the conditions under the clearance. Now, all you have to do it to pay the amount agreed against which you'll get the licenses that you will add to your chain of title.

The chain of title is the place where your licensing will remain, as it will later be needed in case you need to take an Errors &

Omissions insurance (E&O) or your sales agent requires it.

So, one thing is the song.

Another thing is the recording of it.

## PUBLISHING RIGHTS

Joanne Goldenvoice wrote a song called "Beautiful Song". She records it in her room while playing a guitar and uploads it to YouTube.

As the AUTHOR of the song, she owns the PUBLISHING COPYRIGHT.

Because she recorded the song herself (and paid for it), she also owns the MASTER COPYRIGHT of her recording (master) of the song.

## MASTER RIGHTS

Mick Jaguar listens to the song on YouTube and loves it. His band The Rolling Pebbles decides to record their own version of "Beautiful Song" for their upcoming album.

Because Joanne Goldenvoice owns the publishing copyright, the band pays her royalties in order to obtain a license to record their own version of her song.

They perform, create and produce a new recording: a NEW MASTER.

The Rolling Pebbles now own the MASTER COPYRIGHT for this new version, but the PUBLISHING COPYRIGHT remains with Joanne Goldenvoice (the original author) as well as the MASTER COPYRIGHT of her recording (made by her).

By now we have ONE song belonging to its composer and TWO masters belonging to different entities.

## USAGE RIGHTS

Martino Scorsese is making a film about green giraffes and is a big fan of the Rolling Pebbles. He wants to use their version of "Beautiful Song" in his film.

The producer of the film has to pay The Rolling Pebbles in order to obtain a MASTER USE LICENSE to use their recording (their master) of the song.

He also has to pay Joanne Goldenvoice in order to obtain a SYNCHRONIZATION LICENSE for the song "Beautiful Song" whose PUBLISHING COPYRIGHT she owns. Because it's her song.

It's called Publishing COPYRIGHT because only the person(s) who wrote/composed the song has the power to grant you an authorization (license) that will allow you to COPY it as a new version of that song.

It's called Master COPYRIGHT because only the person OR company that owns that recording of the song has the power to grant you an authorization (license) to USE it in a new work you will own.

Here are just a few examples of songs, their writers, the publishers, the performers of those songs, the masters that were produced and the record labels that own or control the masters.

| SONG | WRITTEN BY | PUBLISHED BY | PERFORMED BY | ON A MASTER OWNED BY | RECORD LABEL |
|------|-----------|-------------|-------------|---------------------|-------------|
| "Michelle" | John Lennon/Paul McCartney | Sony/ATV | The Beatles | "Michelle" | Parlophone |
| "Something" | George Harrison | Harrisongs | The Beatles | "Something" | Parlophone |
| Walk on By" | Burt Bacharach/Hal David | Carlin Music Corp. | Dionne Warwick | "Walk on By" | Scepter Records |
| "You've Got a Friend" | Carole King | Screen Gems/Columbia | Carole King | "You've Got a Friend" | Ode/A&M Records |
| "What'd I Say" | Ray Charles | Universal Music | Ray Charles | "What'd I Say" | Atlantic Records |
| "Stella by Starlight" | Ned Washington/Victor Young | Famous Music | Ray Charles | "Stella by Starlight" | Ray Charles Enterprises |
| "Gimme Shelter" | Mick Jagger/Keith Richards | ABKCO Music | The Rolling Stones | "Gimme Shelter" | ABKCO Records |

A song is born when a composer writes it.

A master is born when THREE entities meet: a COMPOSITION, a RECORDING ARTIST and a RECORD LABEL. The first one was created by the writer of the music and lyrics while the second is the people who perform that composition. We are calling them "recording artists" and not just "performers" because we want to emphasize the fact that there is a recording of the performance going on – and not just a performance that may be lost if no one records it.

The Record Label is usually the entity that not just brought the composition and the recording artist together, but also hired the musicians, booked and paid for countless studio sessions, handles the marketing, makes the discs (or any other medium) and, therefore, OWNS or CONTROLS such master.

Sometimes, the composer and recording artist are the same person, like Carole King regarding "You've Got a Friend"; a song she wrote herself and performed herself for her own album "Tapestry". Sometimes the composer and the recording artist are two completely separate people like Burt Bacharach and Hal David (composers) who wrote "I Say a Little Prayer" for Dionne Warwick to record.

There are also cases where the composer and the recording artist only partially match. Although "Something" is a song recorded by The Beatles for their album "Abbey Road", it was written only by one of them: George Harrison, while other Beatles songs like "Michelle" was written by two other Beatles, John Lennon and Paul McCartney.

Let's say it again: keep in mind that a recording you like always has two dimensions:

The music composition (from which the composer gets the

publishing rights)

The recording of it (the master that belongs to whoever paid for it – be the performing artist or a record label).

Each one of these belongs to or is controlled by an entity (a person or a company). You will need to obtain the rights to both if you want a specific song in your film.

## PUBLISHING RIGHTS

Dolly Parton wrote "I Will Always Love You" and recorded the song in 1974.

As the writer, she owns the publishing copyright of the song.

The master she recorded for her album is (today) owned by Sony Music (through its sub-label Legacy Recordings) that owns RCA Records, the record label under whose contract Dolly Parton was when she recorded the song.

## MASTER RIGHTS

Whitney Houston, in 1992, decided to record a new version of the song.

For that to happen, royalties were paid to Dolly Parton (the writer who has the publishing copyright) in exchange for the license that allowed Whitney Houston's recording of it.

The Whitney Houston recording of the song is a new master – this one owned by Arista Records.

## USAGE RIGHTS

In the film THE BODYGUARD (1992), in order for the Whitney Houston master to be used, producers had to pay Arista Records for the master use license.

They also had to pay a synchronization fee to Dolly Parton (who owns the publishing copyright of the song) in order to get a synchronization license.

Without both the master Use license and the synchronization license, the song cannot be used.

*So, the lesson number two is this: the combination of people that give birth to the song (or the recording) you want to use is very diverse and you should not think that just because there is only one person singing on the CD, it means there is only one person to talk to when the time comes to put that song in your film.*

To whoever owns the publishing copyright, the producer needs to pay a synchronization fee in order to obtain a synchronization license.

To whoever owns the master recording, the producer needs to pay a master use fee in order to obtain a master use license.

A similar thing happened with "I'm Every Woman" (Ashford/Simpson).

## PUBLISHING RIGHTS
## + FIRST MASTER

Nickolas Ashford and Valerie Simpson wrote the song "I'm Every Woman" that was recorded in 1978 by Chaka Khan for her solo debut album "Chaka".

Because they are the writers, Ashford & Simpson own the publishing copyright over the song.

The Chaka Khan master belongs to Warner Bros. Records., under whose contract Chaka Khan was at the time.

## A SECOND MASTER

The song was covered in 1992 by Whitney Houston for the soundtrack of film THE BODYGUARD that was, in fact, a Whitney Houston album.

This master belongs to Arista Records under whose contract Whitney Houston was at the time, and for it to exist, the record label must have paid Ashford & Simpson for a license that allowed Whitney to record her version of their song.

## USAGE RIGHTS OVER THE SECOND MASTER

In the film THE BODYGUARD (1992), in order for the Whitney Houston master to be used, producers had to pay Arista Records for the master use license.

They also had to pay a synchronization fee to Ashford & Simpson (who own the publishing copyright of the song) in order to get a synchronization license.

Without both the master Use license and the synchronization license, the song cannot be used.

## USAGE RIGHTS OVER THE
## FIRST MASTER

In the film THE 40 YEAR-OLD VIRGIN (2005) the Chaka Khan version of the song appears.

For that to happen, the producers had to pay Warner Bros. Records for a master use license of Chaka Khan's 1978 master.

They also had to pay a synchronization fee to Ashford & Simpson (who own the publishing copyright of the song) in order to get a synchronization license.

Without both the master use license and the synchronization license, the song cannot be used.

The next images will explain, in broad terms, how the music business works. Its complexity comes from the many forms licenses and royalties circulate and the different sides of the business that are handled by different entities.

Basically, the music business is divided into FOUR different branches:
1 - Composing
2 - Performance
3 - Publishing/Licensing
4 - Recording

COMPOSING means the creative business of writing songs – music and lyrics – be them for records, advertising, movies, theatre and any medium that needs music.

PERFORMANCE means the artistic business of public performance of any kind of music – be it live or reproduced by mechanical means. It is done the by the Artist.

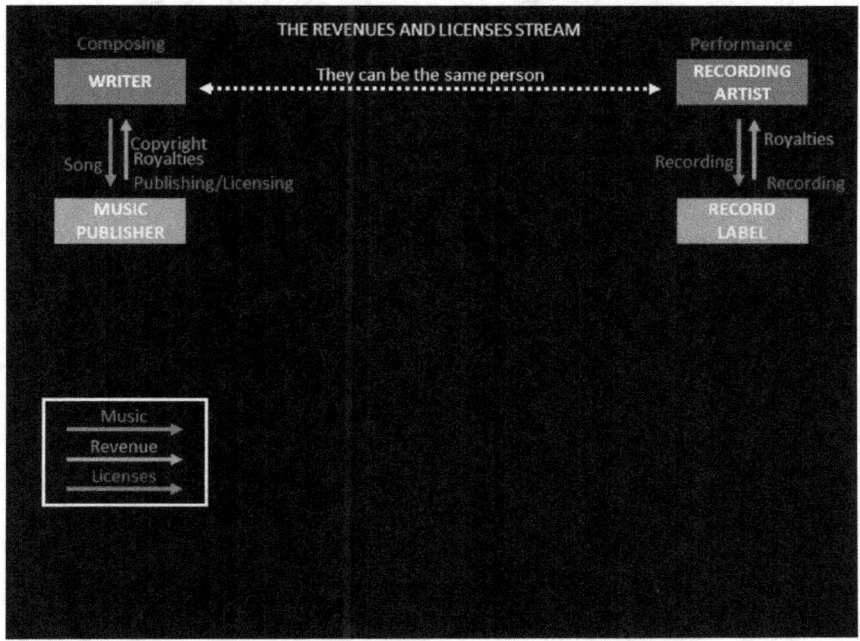

PUBLISHING/LICENSING means the business of managing a catalog of previously composed music through the careful decision-making regarding HOW they can be licensed to every possible use or medium.

RECORDING means the creative business of producing masters that can be mass reproduced and sold to listeners and fans of the artists. It also includes the marketing and the distribution of those recordings. It also includes the licensing of any usage rights pertaining those masters.

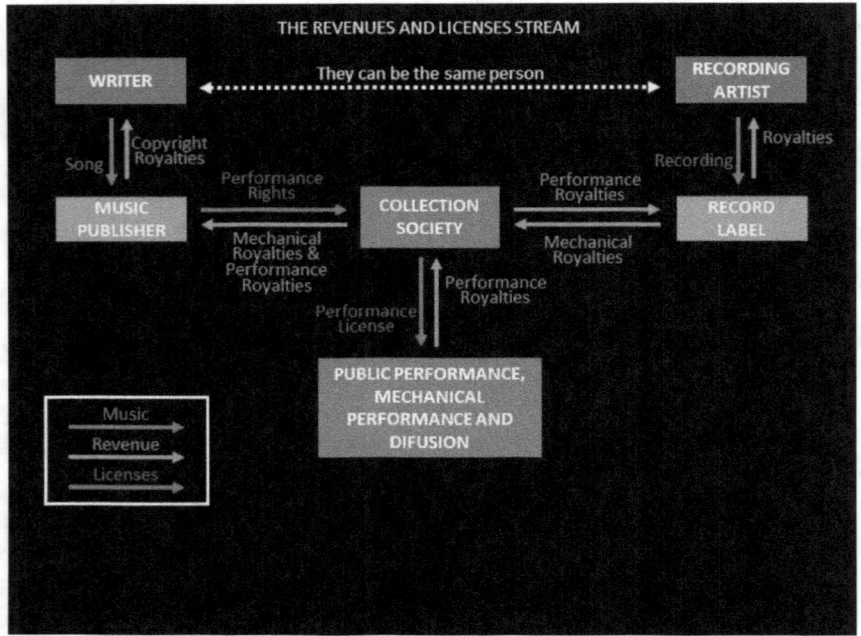

·As you can see through the image, SOME uses are administered through collection societies:

- Mechanical performances in restaurants, elevators, gyms, supermarkets, etc.,
- Mechanical performances on radio,
- Live performances and shows,
- The compilation of different masters that are released together on CDs like "Hits from the 60's",
- Uses on web applications, ringtones, etc.,
- The production of cover versions.

The use of music in films, TV, games and other audiovisual media is NOT usually included in the scenario above. Those uses are handled separately unless the rights owners expressly tell you to go through a collection society.

What is a collection society and why we don't use them?

Collection Societies are entities (private or public) whose main business is to represent copyright holders when it comes to authorizing and monitoring the use of their work, setting prices for the many uses and collecting revenues. Keep in mind that in just one country, one song can be played on multiple radio stations, public places like bars and restaurants, broadcast on a TV show or sold on compilation CDs. Lyrics can be reproduced in magazines and the whole song can be performed live at weddings, concerts or just re-recorded for ringtones.

Such types of business are too frequent to be brought to a music publisher or a record label. Yet, they can generate a lot of money. That's why copyright holders sign up with collections societies all over the world and allow the collecting of revenues to flow through them. Inside their countries, those collection societies reign supreme: they will do (or enforce) whatever the Copyright Laws allow them to do. Some of them are specialized in music. Some are specialized in only one kind of music. Some will equally handle other media (like Literature and Art). Others will not do music at all.

Every country has at least one collection society. The USA has more than ten: ASCAP and BMI are the biggest. The UK has PRS for Music, Germany has GEMA, France has SACEM, Portugal has SPA, etc.

What about film?

The key issue here is that the licensing of music for audiovisual works tends to bypass the collection societies and go direct to the records labels and publishers – and those copyright holders expect just that. Why? Because licensing a music into a film is not as innocuous or automatic as playing it on a radio or allowing someone to sing it on a wedding. Contrary to most uses that have an ephemeral nature, film stays. The use of music on a film can change the music and the artist as much as it changes the film. That's why copyrights holders want to look at it personally.

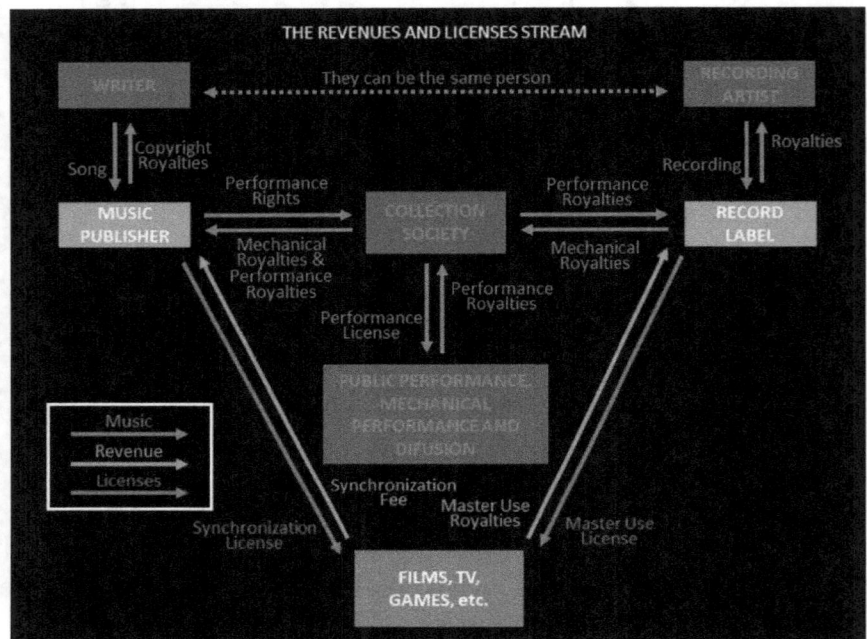

And because the royalties and fees involved can be substantial, film producers want to make sure they are talking to the right people and not to a collection society that, sometimes, does not care.

The music publisher (the entity that rules the composition) will be the one to license the reproduction and commercial distribution of the song to music sheet publishers.

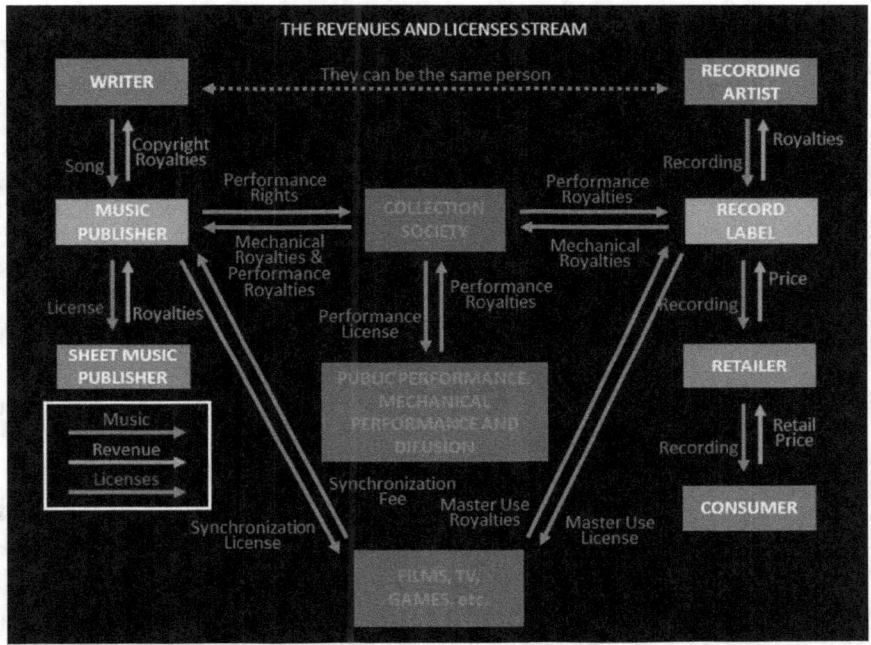

The record label (the entity that rules the master recording) will be in charge of designing the package, duplication, marketing, distribution (to retailers) and everything regarding CDs, MP3 files, Vinyl records, etc. to be sold to consumers.

As a rule of thumb, the more inconsequential the licensing (regardless of how much money it makes), the more those entities (publisher and record label) will rely on collection societies who will handle the massive amount of requests from all over the world – and collect the money upfront.

And here is the whole landscape, in its full glory.

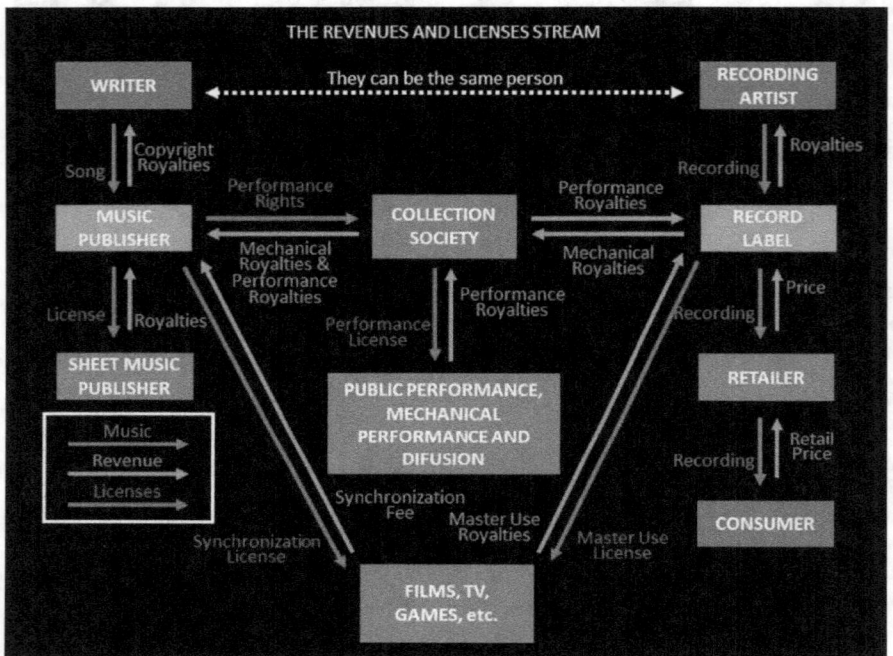

Now comes the hard part.

For every creative or intellectual work that goes into a particular product (in this case, a song) there is the potential for the ownership of that right. Why is this important? Because only the person who owns a right (over something he/she created, wrote, performed, paid for etc.) can ultimately grant you the permission to use that song (in your film) and set the price for it.

So, if you think about a song that was written by two people and performed by a third person, you have potentially three people to talk to (and pay) before being able to put that song in your film.

From all that was said above, we can identify two separate elements: the musical COMPOSITION (that comes from the composer's work) and the PERFORMANCE of that composition. The composition may have several composers and owners and the performer may also be a completely different set of people. Billy Joel's "New York State of Mind" was performed by himself for his own album and later covered by other artists like Barbra Streisand and Carmen McRae.

Depending on what version of the song you want, you will have to consider talking to different people. The composer will rarely ever change, while the performer varies according to which version are you talking about: Joel's, Streisand's or McRae's.
We mentioned the master. What is the master?

The master is the studio RECORDING properly mixed and ready to be distributed.

So... John Fogerty wrote "Bad Moon Rising" that was performed/recorded by Creedence Clearwater Revival. If you want to see a great use for that song in a film, just check AN AMERICAN WEREWOLF IN LONDON (1981). In order to be sold to us and enjoyed by us, that composition and the performance had to be fixated in a specific recording. If something is not recorded, well, it is lost and has no use for us. That recording is called the master.

*So, lesson number three is: always try to identify the complete set of people (or companies) you will have to talk to at the same time in order to get the permission to use the song you want. You will have to identify each one of them because if one of them stays out or simply says "no", then you have a problem.*

The master will later be copied (duplicated) in CDs, MP3 files, vinyl records and etc. Those copies will be sold to us by retailers like Amazon, Best Buy, iTunes, Fnac, etc.

So… a copy of the master is what we are listening to at home or in the car: the recording of the performance of the song, sold to us in a specific format (CD, digital file, LP, etc.).

Typically, the master is owned by a RECORD LABEL and kept in a very safe place. The record label is usually the entity that paid for that recording session, the artists, the musicians, the marketing, the music video, the production of the CDs, the packaging of the CDs, the distribution, etc.

The record label made it all happen… so it typically owns the master.

The Studio master is important because it is the definitive, immortal, singular version of a certain song. Usually it is the version we all know and the version that appears in the artist's album (that is basically a copy of a collection of masters).

Think about Madonna's "Material Girl" (written by Peter Brown and Robert Rans), the song that opens the album "Like a Virgin". Of course the song has been performed live many times or covered by other artists. However, that master from 1984 is the version we all have in our minds.

The "Material Girl" master is owned by Sire Records (that in turn, is owned by Warner Bros. Records).

There may be other masters of the same song (covers performed by other artists). However, this particular master has a considerable value because it is highly evocative of many things: the era, the artist, the sound of the 80's… and ourselves in those days – it's hard to think about 1984 and not to remember when we were young and listening to what was one of the hottest songs of that year.

It is that evocative nature that this master brings to a film whose story is set in 1984. Put that song playing on teenagers listening to a Walkman and immediately a whole era is set. No other master of that song will give you the instant recognition. No other version of the song has such power to connect with the audience.

By now, we hope you understand the different roles played by COMPOSERS, RECORDING ARTISTS and RECORD LABELS. You Also know what a MASTER is.

Bear in mind that through decades the whole music industry has built its business model upon the production, distribution and commerce of these moments when the composer (with his/her talent for writing great melodies and lyrics) and the artist (with his/her amazing voice, presence, personality) get bound forever in timeless masters.

Over the years, record labels like Motown, Atlantic, Columbia, Warner, Verve, EMI, Decca, Island, Def Jam, RCA Victor, Tamla, Philadelphia International, Salsoul, Parlophone, and so many others, accumulated dozens of thousands of masters made/paid by them. And as they went along, bigger labels bought smaller ones; complex deals were made and the result was that to us, outsiders, identifying who owns what can be a bit tricky.

*Lesson number four is: beyond selecting the song you want and identifying its composers and performers, you also have to identify who owns that particular master you want to use and add them to the list of people/companies you will have to ask for permission.*

## 2 – RELATIONSHIPS REGARDING COMPOSERS, ARTISTS AND LABELS

Earlier, we identified COMPOSERS (the owners of the publishing rights of a song), ARTISTS (performers of the song) and RECORD LABELS (the owner of the recording of it all) as the entities you should talk to whenever you select one song you want to use in your film. This is the typical trinity that should be your guide through the process.

However, there are some lessons we can extract from practice.

It gets a bit trickier if all you have is a pirated music file you obtained from an illegal source (like a website). Keep in mind that in many of those cases, the composers' names are missing, the artist's name is wrong and even the titles of the songs themselves are wrong. There are many examples. In 1974, singer/songwriter William DeVaughn recorded the hit song "Be Thankful for What You've Got" for Roxbury Records.

*Lesson number five: in most cases, the official CD will contain the basic identification of those persons and companies. Look inside the booklet or on the small print on the CD label face itself. It is usually there. From that, you just have to figure out the way to get to the right people. Usually, your best starting point is calling the record label office (if you are in the same country as the origin of the master), the record label in your country that represents the original record label or the nearest collection society (there is at least one in every country) that collects royalties on behalf of artists.*

Because he never got to be a big name and because his voice sounds like Curtis Mayfield, lots of people assume the song is by Curtis Mayfield. Plus, many people think the song's name is "Diamond in the Back" since those words are repeated many times in the main refrain (and it's very catchy). The result? It is not hard to download an illegal MP3 file of "Diamond in the Back" by Curtis Mayfield – especially if the file comes from Europe or Asia, where knowledge about American soul music from the 70's varies a lot. This specific example comes from a Portuguese radio station that played the song for months(!) and named it just like that.

You should also take into consideration that the relationship between recording artists and record labels, many times is not what it seems. Although we said before that recording artists also have rights, therefore, they are a part of the trinity, many times, contractual conditions – especially when the artist is small and unknown – exclude them from any business that comes after the creation of the master. What happens here is that some record labels practice a flat fee for the artist's work. In 1958, Nina Simone was paid a flat fee of $3000.00 for her work on her first album "Little Girl Blue" for Bethelehem Records. In that album, you'll find one of her biggest hits, "My Baby Just Cares for Me" (Donaldson/Kahn). Nina Simone was at least the 10th performer to record the song (it has been recorded by many artists since the 30's). Ms. Simone's version wasn't a big hit until 1987 when Chanel used it on a TV commercial for its Chanel n°5 perfume. That use of the master in a commercial (and the single's re-release that took place) generated millions in royalties that went to the record label and the composers. Not a dime for the performer.

# 3 – TWO EXAMPLES: ABBEY ROAD AND RAY OF LIGHT

Over the next pages, you'll see a breakdown of the information found on the booklet of the album "Abbey Road" (1969) by The Beatles – we'll be using the 2009 remaster edition – and a deeper breakdown of the song "Ray of Light" by Madonna, from her album "Ray of Light" (1998). The goal is to dig a little deeper into the meaning of the information provided and learn how it can help you get what you are looking for.

ABOUT "ABBEY ROAD"

This publisher controls the Lennon/McCartney songs.

This publisher controls the two songs by George Harrison

This publisher controls the one song by Ringo Starr

All songs published by Sony/ATV Music Publishing LLC except tracks 2 and 7, Harrisongs Ltd and 5, Startling Music Ltd.

This remaster is protected since it was produced in 2009 and should not be confused with the "older and inferior-sounding" master previously available.

Who owns this remaster? Who can authorize anything and everything regarding this remaster?

Ye bitches, we say it again, so get this through your thick skull!

Digital Remaster ℗ 2009 The copyright of this sound recording is owned by EMI Records Ltd. © EMI Records Ltd.
This label copy information is the subject of copyright protection. All rights reserved.

Even this information is protected just in case you copy these recordings or do your version of these songs – or anything! You have to ask the entities identified above!

Not just some. ALL! Nothing is left out! Nothing! Zero! It's all ours!

Artwork © 2009 Apple Corps. Ltd. All photographs © Apple Corps Ltd.

The original artwork contained in the original album has been upgraded for this re-release (or it's new), so there is a new copyright here.

All the photos are also protected.

# ABOUT "RAY OF LIGHT"

The legal information about the publishing of the song "Ray of Light" by Madonna from her album "Ray of Light" (1998) reads:

Written by Madonna, William Orbit, Clive Maldoon, Dave Curtis and Christine Leach.
© 1998 WB Music Corp./ Webo Girl Publishing Inc. admin. by WB Music Corp. ASCAP/Rondor Music (London), Limited PRS
All Rights Adm. by Almo Music Corp. ASCAP in the U.S./Canada /Purple Music Limited PRS

Now let's break it:

Written by Madonna, William Orbit, Clive Muldoon, Dave Curtis and Christine Leach.

DAMN! That's a lot of writers!

© 1998 WB Music Corp./ Webo Girl Publishing Inc. admin. by WB Music Corp. ASCAP/Rondor Music (London), Limited PRS

All Rights Adm. by Almo Music Corp. ASCAP in the U.S./Canada /Purple Music Limited PRS

Because four of the five writers are British (but the American one is still the biggest), it's important to note that the credits make sure we understand which company handles what in both countries. ASCAP is the American collection society while Rondor Music and PRS (today PRS for Music) do the same in the UK.

Madonna's RAY OF LIGHT is a song based on a song based on a song. In 1971, the British folk duo Curtiss Maldoon (Dave Curtis and Clive Maldoon) released a song titled SEPHERYN. The publishing of that song is controlled by Purple Music. Christine Leach (Maldoon's niece) rewrote the song into RAY OF LIGHT with William Orbit. Regarding their part of the composition, these two artists bring in a new publisher: Rondor Music (a publishing arm of A&M Records created for handling UK music, while a sister company, Almo Music, does something similar in North America). When Madonna enters the picture, she adds her own changes to the song, thus bringing her own publisher into the scene: Webo Girl Publishing Inc.

All this is administered by one entity: WB Music Corp.

Although we do not know the split between the four parties, it's safe to assume that, being the most powerful artist, it is Madonna who takes a bigger share (in relative terms) and puts her record company and her publisher on the key decision-making position.

While the publishing information in the Madonna album has to appear song by song on the booklet due the large number of different writers, the information regarding those masters (the album contains 13) is the same:

Maverick Records Company. Marketed by Warner Bros. Records Inc.
© ℗ Warner Bros. Records Inc.
Unauthorized copying, hiring, lending, public performance and broadcasting of this record is prohibited!

Now let's break it:

Maverick Records Company. Marketed by Warner Bros. Records Inc.

Madonna's own record label (at that time) Maverick Records is the owner of these masters. All of them? Yes, since there is no other information saying otherwise. Warner Bros. Records only handles the marketing and distribution.

© ℗ Warner Bros. Records Inc.

The © and ℗ symbols appear together frequently on records. We also saw them on ABBEY ROAD. The difference between them is simple: ℗ is a sound recording copyright symbol (meaning it's referring specifically to the master) while the © refers to everything (the 13 music compositions, the reproduction of the lyrics on the booklet, artwork, etc.) and also the master. So the name next to the © symbol tells you exactly who to contact in case you want that master recording on your film. But there's more: although Maverick owns the masters, the symbols next to Warner Bros. Records tells us they also act, protect, control and collect on behalf of Maverick.

Unauthorized copying, hiring, lending, public performance and broadcasting of this record is prohibited!

Exactly what it says.

*Lesson number six: once you correctly establish communication with the record label about a specific master, try to understand who are the people and companies (between composers and artists) who have any power of decision.*

Sometimes the artist has lots of power and can say "no" (or ask for a lot of money). Sometimes they have no power and do not even get paid. Sometimes they do get paid through the record label who's the one making all the decision regarding a specific master. Sometimes the record label will even decide in the name of the composer. Sometimes, the composers' rights are completely separated from the record label (and you'll have to ask them individually). Sometimes there are two record labels: one deciding for the master and a second one that decides through the composer.

If the artist writes his/her own stuff, is very small and has never released anything, then it is
possible that he/she can grant you the permissions you need regarding composition and the master. Bear in mind that this is the reality with many newcomers. Today's technology is so amazing that virtually anyone who's starting now can have a recording studio in a bedroom and produce his/her own masters (and grant you the permissions you need). But if you want U2's "Sunday Bloody Sunday", that's a whole different game.

*Lesson number seven: bigger and smaller artists and composers have different relationships and contractual rights/obligations. Every master represents a specific relationship between rights owners that you must understand in order to negotiate a good deal.*

## 4 – WHO AND WHAT ARE WE LOOKING FOR?

Composers are usually connected to PUBLISHING COMPANIES. The music publishing business is very old and basically comes from the times when music was commercialized under the form of sheet music – long before the invention of the technology of sound recording and reproduction. In those days if you wanted to listen to a song, you'd have to buy the music sheet and play it yourself at home or attend a live performance. Back then, composers would license their music to publishers pretty much in the same way writers
(of novels) still get published today. In fact, the two businesses were deeply related, since both mediums relied heavily on the same printed format: a book (with either text or musical notes). However, as recording technology arrived, slowly the music publishing business started to split itself into two different domains: the original business of publishing music sheet and the business of managing the composers' publishing rights (to any media – including the original business of publishing music sheet).

If you look, for example, at the booklet inside the Beatles album "Abbey Road" you'll see who are the publishing companies behind the compositions in the album:

- Sony/ATV Music Publishing LLC for the Lennon/McCartney songs,
- Harrisongs for the two George Harrison songs,
- Startling Music Ltd. for the only Ringo Star's song in the album.

The master, however, (or the digital remaster) belongs to a completely different entity:

- EMI Records Ltd. (now part of the Universal Music Group)

This means that if you want to use "Here Comes the Sun" in your film, you will have to ask EMI Records Ltd. (that owns the master you will be using) and Harrisongs (that represents the composer who wrote the song). If, instead, you want to use "Come Together", you still have to ask EMI Records Ltd., but because this is a Lennon/McCartney song, the publisher is different: Sony/ATV Music Publishing LLC.

This means that composers' side of the trinity is usually handled through a publishing company that manages his/her publishing rights. If you do not know what entity has the authority over the publishing of a certain song, you can ask the record label. They should know, since for the master to exist, the record label must have paid them (the publishers) – otherwise there would be no master to begin with. That's why the record label is your best point of entry to it all.

*Lesson number eight: if the song you want is from an album, you will have to get the permission (or clearance) from at least two entities: the owner of the master and who controls the publishing. As it was said before, sometimes a record label can do it all (because they control it all); sometimes it can't. Sometimes, you will have to talk to ten different people. It all depends on what was written on the contracts between all the people (composers, artists or musicians) that created the master.*

Licensing is a very lucrative business. Over the decades, bigger record labels bought not just smaller record labels, but also, bought hundreds of publishing companies that were created by composers. This is the reality regarding the three biggest labels in the world: Universal Music, Warner Bros. and Sony Music. If they control the master, there is a big chance they also control the publishing – especially with smaller or older artists.

Ray Charles was one of the first artists who changed this. At a certain point, he became so big that he decided he wanted to own the masters and not let the label be the one to profit from the master and its licensing. So, there is this tendency for bigger, powerful artists to own more, while pushing the record labels into smaller roles. Madonna created

Maverick Records in 1992 as the company that would control the masters and anything related to her. She also created her own publisher: Webo Girl Publishing inc.

Now let's discuss what are the rights you are asking for.

Typically, what you need in order to have a song in your film are:
- A master use license (for the specific master recording you want to use);
- A synchronization license (for the composition in question).

The master use license is what you need from whoever controls the master (the recording), while the synchronization license is granted by who controls the publishing (the song itself). While the license for the master use is an obvious thing, the term "synchronization" may seem odd. However, it comes from 20's when film stopped being silent and started to have synch sound. So, the license you get is for synchronizing frames and music as you need – a specificity of the film medium. Later, when TV came along, the term naturally included it, since, well, TV images have pretty much the same nature as film when it comes to its need for synch sound. Much later, came video games and, again, the license remained the same. So, regardless if you are making a film, a television soap opera or a video game, once you decide you want a Madonna song synched with it, you'll need a synchronization license from the publisher.

Now that you understand where the term "synchronization" comes from, here's another one, just for the sake of curiosity, that's even older: "mechanical rights" (check again the "Revenues and Licenses Stream" image to see it). It's the rights you'll need to obtain in case you want to play some music in a public place like a restaurant, the lobby of a movie theater or an elevator. It comes from a time when there was a mechanical device playing a vinyl record, a tape or a CD. The funny thing is that it's still called "mechanical" although music nowadays is played on devices that are digital and not mechanical.

## 5 – DURATION, TERRITORIES, FORMATS AND USES

Ok, so you managed to correctly identify the people/companies you must talk to in order to obtain the master use license and the synchronization license that will give you the clearance to go and use the song you want. In that dialogue there will be two classes of questions that you must answer to all the parties that will grant (or deny) you the licenses you need. The first is a group of objective questions that have to do with the license itself (what you are asking for). The second is a group of subjective questions that have to do with the film itself and how it may affect the song and vice-versa (the "how" it will be used).

The objective group is:
A – Term/duration of the license;
B – Territories where the license is valid;
C – Media formats on which the film will be shown.

The subjective group is composed of any concern the owners of the rights may have regarding your film. They can be anything. However, the most typical are:
1 – The nature of the film;

2 – The nature of the scene where the song will be used;
3 – How many times the song is played on the film;
4 – How many seconds will be played;
5 – Will there be any alterations to the song;
6 – Will there be any addition to the song;
7 – What is your film budget;
8 – What is your film budget for music?
9 – Who's in the film.
10 – Do they like the project?

The first group is fairly simple. This is an objective and cumulative group: the more you want, the more you pay. This means this group is all about calculating the PRICE.

A – The term/duration of the license has to do with how many years you need the music to be in the film. You may save money and ask for one year or two. You may prefer to ask for 20 years or perpetuity. Of course, the price asked will not be the same so you have to fully understand what you need. Sometimes you are producing an art-house film that will play in festivals only and probably will not have a significant international distribution. In that case, it may be easier (and cheaper) to ask for two years, which is the time during which you will be submitting your film to festivals. There is no need to pay for 20 years if in those 20 years the circulation of your film with be extremely limited. Of course, if you ask for perpetuity, that means that film and music will be forever bound together and it will never be taken off. It is a guaranteed way to not have problems. However, it will cost a lot more. If you are unsure, you can ask the rights owner to set, in writing, the price of term extensions should you need them (in case your film unexpectedly gets selected by Cannes and ends up winning the Palme d'Or). If all goes well and you feel your film is in for the long run, you already know what the prices will be for 10, 20 years or perpetuity (then all you have to do is pay). A possible strategy is to pay for two or five years and then if the film still has some distribution here and there, replace the song for something cheaper (save money while still being able to sell the film). That may save some money on rights, but make you spend some more on new deliverables. You have to pay attention to this issue upfront.

B – By territories, we mean the number of countries where your film will be commercially available with that song in it. You can start with your own country (the most obvious market for your film). However, your licenses must specify other countries if the film will be distributed there. The most accepted way is to identify countries by their official name or simply "the whole world". You can also (this is not a joke) add "the entire universe" to the contract. This makes sense if you think that 50 years from now someone in a hotel in Mars may like to watch your film. Again, the more territories, the more expensive those licenses will be. Avoid negotiating territories based on other generic/uncertain criteria like continent (is Turkey a part of Europe?) or debatable criteria such as language (you are trying to get German speaking countries, but not all of Switzerland speaks German; and although there are German speaking communities in the south of Brazil, you won't be able to convince anyone that Brazil is included). Again, you can ask the rights holder to write the price for other countries and so on. This way you'll know how much it will cost you the moment a foreign distributor wants your film.

C – By media formats we are talking about the possible formats that will carry your film (where the music will be). Are you releasing your film in theaters? In which format? A 35mm print? A DCP? Then what comes after? Video on Demand? Streaming? DVD? Blu-ray? VHS? Super VHS? Betamax? ED-Beta? Laserdisc? Hi-8 tapes? Super-8? Video2000? VideoCD? CD-Interactive? HD-DVD? One may laugh when confronted with so many obsolete formats that obviously will never be used. However, keep in mind that these formats represent only 40 years of a film's life. This means that in the next 40 years, many more formats may appear that we haven't heard of yet.

Why would we? They haven't been invented yet. The truth is: once you get the specific license covering only what you think is relevant today (DCP, DVD, Blu-ray and Video on Demand, TV), you are not just closing the door on past obsolete formats, but also leaving future formats equally outside of your license. That was exactly the problem that happened to thousands of titles (films and TV shows) that could not be released on DVD since their music licenses (made during the seventies or earlier) did not cover that new format (they covered VHS and that was it). The result? Many films and TV series had to wait years until their producers could renew (pay) those licenses in order to make them cover DVD and future formats. Some producers could never renew those licenses (for reasons of price or availability) and simply had to put different, cheaper music for DVD and future releases. Sacrilege? Yes, but that's what happens if you don't think about future formats – and one would be surprised on how many films' music soundtracks we enjoy today on, say, VOD, do not match the soundtrack from the VHS release 30 years ago!

Plus, you may believe that a certain format is dead when it is far from it! If your film is an official co-production with France, then your French co-producer probably must deliver a 35mm print of the film to CNC for archive purposes. Your music should be there too. Tip: when in doubt, a good sales agent is the perfect person to tell you what are the formats currently en vogue in most territories.

The key here is the same as with term and territories: to think strategically. Nowadays, because the number of distribution platforms is ever changing and growing, the safest way is to include in the license something like "all formats available today and to be invented in the future". But again, this will have an impact in the cost. If you feel your project will not have a long life, save your money. If you are unsure and have little money now, ask for the price of all formats in writing so you'll already know the price once you get there.

A possible way to save money here is to ask for a worldwide non-commercial license (often called a "Festival License") that will limit the showing of the film to festivals only (if your strategy allows it). That way you'll feel the terrain through festivals before paying licenses for commercial release. This is a special license covering A, B and C that will allow you one year for festival screening (worldwide) in any format the festival uses. Very simple.

Contrary to the previous group that was all about calculating PRICE, the subjective group of issues is not so easy to put a finger on because this group is about calculating VALUE (for you, for the song and for the rights' holders). Here, getting the license you need depends on the PERCEPTION of the rights' owner regarding your film. Of course, that will have an impact on price. One of the main concerns is if the use of a certain song in a film will be detrimental to the song itself, to the artist and in what ways this licensing will contribute to a value increase or decrease regarding the song, the artist and his/her entire catalog. Some artists just simply refuse any licensing because, well, go figure. Always remember that film and music are at the core of the creative industries. So, we're talking about Art here. It may be THE TEENAGE MUTANT NINJA TURTLES to you, but still Art and the juxtaposing of two works together (a film and a song) may affect the individual value of both.

In a way, that is easy to understand. Artists like The Beatles, The Doors, U2, Led Zeppelin, Bruce Springsteen, Joy Division, Eagles, Pink Floyd or ABBA have achieved such a stratospheric status that they know they will get flooded with all types of requests (most of them lousy) the minute they open the gate. Plus, they are in a position where no film, no product and no TV show can do anything for them – with the added risk of angering loyal fans who may hate film X or Z. So they simply say "no" to the licensing of their masters while occasionally allowing the use of covers (you get a synchronization license, but will have to find another version that is not the original).

This means that while it is possible to have Beatles songs in a film, the songs have to be covers, since the studio masters are usually put "off-limits" by EMI, the label that controls them. When was the last time you heard The Beatles' "Yesterday" (the studio master) on a film? We can't remember anything beyond their own film HELP (1965). It's not a matter of money. Exceptions (there are always a few) are their decision to make. The studio masters are the great concern – songs that generations have grown up listening to; songs that evoke a time, a decade, a first kiss, summer. Those are works of art that artists are trying to protect from the damage of a vulgar sex scene, a gore scene or simply an irrelevant scene in an irrelevant film. In the beginning of THE ROYAL TENENBAUMS (2001) it's not Paul McCartney singing "Hey Jude" because although Wes Anderson did manage to get the synchronization license, EMI did not let him have the master use license. He could play the song... but not the original Beatles version we all know and love. If Wes Anderson can't get it, few people can. David Fincher and Aaron Sorkin got it. For the end credits of THE SOCIAL NETWORK, their producers managed to get a master license to "Baby, You're a Rich Man". So, here's an exception.

Disney is another one of those examples of "very hard to get". Try to license "When You Wish Upon a Star" – the real master from PINOCCHIO (1940) – to play during a rape scene. Or try to get "I Want to Be Like You" from THE JUNGLE BOOK (1967) playing as a drug dealer executes an enemy. The answer will be a flat "no". Forget about the rape and the murders! Just try to get those masters for anything. You'll still probably get a "no", since, for Disney, no film is on the level of PINOCCHIO. No other film is worthy... and they do have a point (laughs).

Then there are the picky ones: bands or artists who would license synchronization and master use, but are aiming at bigger contracts like a great Coca-Cola worldwide campaign or the latest Transformers film, and will simply say "no" to smaller films that may scare away bigger business. And that may not be the artist's fault. Many times, managers, parents, label execs – everybody is trying to get the best contracts. Sting couldn't get the radio stations to play his song "Desert Rose". What did he do? He licensed it to car maker Jaguar. Not to a small indie film that played in festivals.

But let's look and the subjective analysis:

1 - The nature of the film is an important issue to rights owners. Is it a horror? Is it a comedy? Is it a big film? A small one? Does it have stars? What distribution will it have? What guarantees are there that it will be worthy? Some "yes" and "no" answers are decided right here when rights holders look at the essence of the film you are producing. They may want to be a part of it or not.

2 - What is the scene where the music will be played? What happens? You will have to describe it in fair detail. Some people may feel tempted to water down anything that might be "an issue". The problem is that describing the scene is just the beginning. The rights owners will eventually hold you accountable to everything that you write. Tell the rights owners, after the film is ready, that the director decided that "explicit sex" was much more interesting that "implied sex" and you may have a big problem. If you feel something on the scene may be of concern, then perhaps the best strategy here would be to be truthful to what the scene is about while also explaining why it is what it is and what value it has for the film. Talk straight and clear here but also feel free to defend the value you are bringing to the screen.

3 – How many times will the song be played on the film is

another big issue. Will it be played only once? Will it be played in scene 10 and later again over the end credits? You may pay premium for repetitions. You pay an even higher premium if the music is to be played over the end credits since it closes the film, thus, setting the mood (or aftertaste) that stays with the audience as the leave the theatre.

4 – How many seconds of the song will be played? Ten? Thirty? This information is important for understanding the impact of a song on scene or sequence. In Tony Scott's THE HUNGER (1983), the Bauhaus classic "Bela Lugosi's Dead" plays over the entire opening sequence. It lasts almost three minutes. It must have cost them a lot – and it works beautifully!

5 – The rights owners will certainly want to know if you are planning to make any alteration to the song. If it's sung by a character, will he/she change the lyrics in any way? If the main character is drugged, will there be a filter over the song in order to simulate his/her point of view? Or if you are using the master, will you change the song's pitch? Or will you cut and rearrange parts of the song to get a longer instrumental part of it? When you ask for a music clearance and you get it, that usually does not come with a license to make changes to it. Be careful and always get pre-clearance on any change of any nature you want to do yourself. On the other hand, you may ask beforehand for alterations to the master that will be supplied to you if it's something you cannot do. You may need for a version of Sinatra's "My Way" with only his voice or just the instrumental. The record label that owns the master can prepare that version specifically for your film. However, this is not easy to obtain and be prepared to pay a big premium. Here, there are no limits to what you can ask… and no limits to what it will cost you.

6 – Will you be adding something to the song? Like the voice of the character singing over the song that's playing on the radio? Or will you do the above and add some new "funny"

lyrics? That will probably cost you another premium (or simply get you a "no").

7 – What is the film's production budget? If they ask, you will have to tell them. Why? Because they will want to know if the budget of the film brings you closer to TITANIC (1997) or CLERKS (1994). Depending on the case, the price they would ask you would not be the same. There will be a connection to the film's budget. The next BATMAN film and a documentary about fishermen in Indonesia are not the same thing – and they know it.

The question above is usually connected with the one below:

8 – What is your budget for music? Typically, on average, a film spends 10%-15% of its budget in music (with exceptions, of course). A Scorsese film like GOODFELLAS (1990) or CASINO (1995) has about 50 (fifty!!) well known songs, each! Go to the end credits and just count them. That is a considerable portion of a film's budget. When discussing rights, the rights owners want to have an idea if you are looking at the music with some fairness and honesty. If your film costs ten million dollars, it would be offensive to be offering $200,00 per master just because the overall music budget is just $800,00. Rights owners will be trying to see if you are not underbudgeting your music – which may destroy your credibility, since a thing of the utmost importance was budgeted like it had no importance at all. On the contrary, if your film is a micro-budget type and still you budgeted its music with care, they might be willing to negotiate a smaller amount for synchronization and master use. Don't lie here. Rights owners usually want to do business and will try to work something out with you – even when you don't have a lot. The only issue here is that if you don't really have a "normal" music budget, you are unlikely to get Madonna (but still rights owners will try to work out alternatives for you). Like in Art, the price of synchronization and master use depends on these

many intangible issues. How much money you've got is just one of them.

9 – Who is in the film? Sometimes, the cast is a deal breaker. If there is no face anyone knows (meaning the film's commercial appeal is limited) it may be harder to get the clearance. But if you have Julia Roberts, it may be easier (and more expensive).

10 – Do they (the people who control the rights) like the project? We left this item for the last because it can overwrite all others. If someone who can say yes or no really likes your project, he/she can make your day and ask little or no money in return. It is your job to present the project and win the heart of that person.

Generally, if you want to get an idea of the type of dialogue you'll be having, just visit – for example – the website of Universal Music. In it (and other music labels have a similar section in their websites) you will find some online forms directed at producers who need music. Many of the questions you'll be answering are exactly the ones we've discussed.

Take a good look at the next images and see what we are talking about.

| Media Type | Advertising ▾ |
| --- | --- |
| Title | Advertising |
| | DVD |
| Territory | Internet |
| | Live Stage |
| # of Songs | Motion Picture |
| | Television |
| Budget | Video Games |
| Paid Online Media | |

# From the Universal Music Group License Request

| | | | | |
|---|---|---|---|---|
| Media Type | Motion Picture ▾ | | | |
| Clearance Person | John Doe | Film Title | "Film Title" | |
| Term | Perpetuity | Territory | Worldwide | |
| Release Date | 07/09/2020 | # of Songs | 1 | |
| Length of Film | 100 minutes | Website | | |
| Publishers | Publishers name | | | |
| Film Budget | 1.000.000 | Music Budget | 100.000 | |
| Timing | Partial ▾ | Duration | 40 seconds | |

☑ Master Used          ☐ Master Cleared

☑ Media Rights         ☐ Re-Record

☐ Film Festival Only   ☐ Theatrical Only

☐ Main Title           ☐ Background Vocal

☐ Lyrics Changed       ☐ Visual Vocal

☐ Parody Lyrics        ☐ Lyrics Displayed

☐ Background Inst.

Synopsis

Scene Description

## Song(s)

| Song Title | Artist | Writers | Actions |
|---|---|---|---|
| | | | ⊞ |

Here's the form you'll see at the Universal Music Licensing Request website. As you can see, it will open the conversation with many of the elements explained before. Note that this form is for the Synchronization License of songs controlled by Universal Music through the many publishers it owns or controls. In many cases they do not control 100% of one song's publishing rights.

| Song Title | Writers | Controlled | Type | ISWC |
|---|---|---|---|---|
| A RAY OF LIGHT<br>UMPG Song Control – 100.0000% | Lalo Schifrin (BMI) | Yes | Original | T-072.083.447-8 |
| ONE RAY OF LIGHT<br>UMPG Song Control – 50.0000% | Howard Russell Smith (ASCAP) (UMPG)\|Susan Longacre (ASCAP) | No | Original | |
| RAY OF LIGHT<br>UMPG Song Control – 100.0000% | Universal Music - MGB Songs (ASCAP) \|Lake-K (UI) | Yes | Original | |
| RAY OF LIGHT<br>UMPG Song Control – 100.0000% | Killer Tracks (BMI) \|Mark Jonathan Russell (PRS) | Yes | Original | T-915.356.301-0 |
| RAY OF LIGHT<br>UMPG Song Control – 10.0000% | Almo Music Corp. (ASCAP) (UMPG) (UMPG)\|William Orbit (PRS) (UMPG)\|Clive Muldoon (PRS) \|Dave Curtiss (PRS) \|Christine Ann Leach (PRS) \|Madonna L. Ciccone (ASCAP) | No | Original | T-070.922.866-9 |

You will ALWAYS have to find out:

1 – Does this rights owner controls 100% of the publishing of the song I want?

2 – If not, who owns the remaining percentages of the song?

From the several songs titled "Ray of Light" whose publishing rights are owned by Universal Music Publishing Group, Madonna's "Ray of Light" is not controlled by this company, since Universal only has 10% of the publishing rights.

However, you still have to pay UMPG, since the 10% it controls is the percentage regarding one of its writers: William Orbit/Almo Music Corp. All other writers are not under the UMPG umbrella. Note that you will always find one of the following scenarios:

1 – This publisher owns 100% of the rights, so it fully controls the publishing license you need.

2 – This publisher does NOT own 100% of the rights, so it does not control the
license you need.

3 – This publisher does NOT own 100% of the rights, but it still controls the license you need.

Sometimes the controlling publisher will speak, decide, price and collect on behalf of all others. Many times, it won't, so you'll have to talk to them yourself, one by one for how many publishers you discover who own a percentage of the song.

Warner/Chappell Music (the music publishing arm of Warner Music Group) will tell you more about the song.

(A) From the list of writers we already know, we understand that Madonna is the one speaking on behalf of the writers. She has the control.

(B) Webo Girl Publishing Inc. and Warner Bros. Music Corp. have the control over the publishing. They control it.

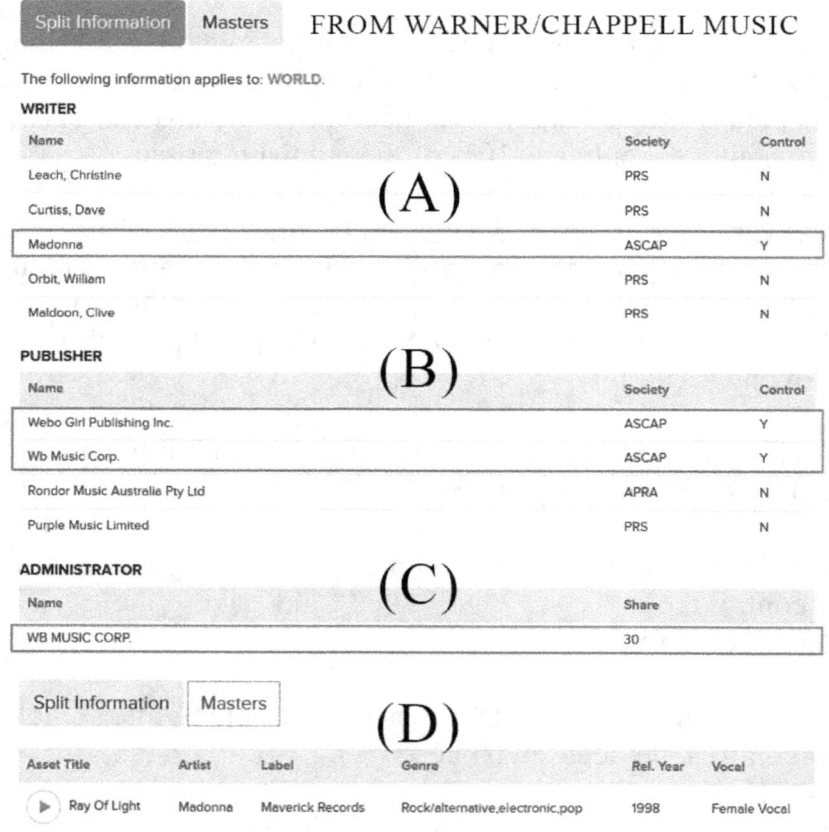

FROM WARNER/CHAPPELL MUSIC

The following information applies to: WORLD.

**WRITER**

| Name | | Society | Control |
|------|------|---------|---------|
| Leach, Christine | | PRS | N |
| Curtiss, Dave | **(A)** | PRS | N |
| Madonna | | ASCAP | Y |
| Orbit, William | | PRS | N |
| Maldoon, Clive | | PRS | N |

**PUBLISHER**

| Name | **(B)** | Society | Control |
|------|------|---------|---------|
| Webo Girl Publishing Inc. | | ASCAP | Y |
| Wb Music Corp. | | ASCAP | Y |
| Rondor Music Australia Pty Ltd | | APRA | N |
| Purple Music Limited | | PRS | N |

**ADMINISTRATOR**

| Name | **(C)** | Share | |
|------|------|-------|---|
| WB MUSIC CORP. | | 30 | |

| Split Information | Masters | **(D)** | | | |
|-------|-------|-------|-------|-------|-------|
| Asset Title | Artist | Label | Genre | Rel. Year | Vocal |
| ▶ Ray Of Light | Madonna | Maverick Records | Rock/alternative,electronic,pop | 1998 | Female Vocal |

(C) And with 30% of the share, it is Warner Bros. Music Corp. that administers the publishing rights.

(D) Through Warner/Chappell Music, you can get to Maverick Records that owns the master of the song – in case you need the Master Use License.

PAULO LEITE

## 6 – HOW ABOUT SOME Q&A?

Sure. Let's start.

**Q: Do I always need to ask for synchronization and master use licenses for my film?**

A: Yes and no. You will need a synchronization license every time you want a song that has a composer who is not under public domain (more on public domain later). He/she who wrote it, owns it. Plain and simple. There is no way to get Visage's "Fade to Grey" without getting the license from Billy Currie, Chris Payne and Midge Ure (its three writers). They may all be represented by one single music publisher that has the power to decide or (worst case) each one of those three writers has his/her own publishing company. Then you'll be talking to all three instead of just one entity. You'll have to find it out (again, the record label should be able to help you). The master use license will be needed only if you want to use that particular recording of the song. If you decide you can play it yourself (making your own version of the song to use in the film), then you will not be needing the master use license, since you are making your own master. But listen to the song… will it be the same to have the master or play it yourself? Only you can decide. Plus, in some cases, the composers will demand the right to approve your version (in case you want to skip an expensive master) and you may end up having to use a master that has been already approved. Be careful.

**Q: But the master is so protected and expensive. What can I do?**

A: Here's a tip: most artists are contractually forbidden (by the record label, when it owns the master) to re-record that song for, say, twenty years. After that, the artist can (and many do) re-record the song imitating to great detail the master from 20 or 30 years ago. To most people the differences are not clear (although they exist). This is particularly true with one-hit-wonders from the 60's, 70's or 80's. Tina Charles had a disco hit in 1976 called "I Love to Love (But My Baby Loves to Dance)". In recent years, she re-recorded the song, thus creating a new master from it. This one, she probably owns and it may cost less than the original 1976 version if you want to use it. Are there audible differences? Of course, but lots of people won't notice the difference (your bank account will). Another tip: check Youtube. Those newer masters are there and you can compare them. They were not created specifically for films. Instead, they were created for cheap album compilations you'll find in gas stations – something like "Big Hits from the 70's" – where a sneaky record label will mix on the same CD some 12 songs: one third of original masters, one third of poorly recorded live performances and one third of those "recreations". Some of those compilations will advertise "original artists" – which is true, however, many of those tracks are not the ones a hardcore fan would be expecting. Most people don't care and are happy just to pay $4,99 for it (wouldn't be that cheap if they used only the original masters). You may take advantage of it. Also, you can check professional copycat bands who are notoriously famous for cashing in the need for recreations of certain masters. This is a business that thrives especially when it comes to older songs (up to the 90's). If you cannot get Adele to sing in your film, you can check several Adele-like singers who specialize in making recordings that sound like her. There are dozens! If we are talking about jazz, for example, keep in mind that several great names like Frank Sinatra, Ella Fitzgerald, Duke Ellington and John Coltrane (just to name a few) recorded multiple versions of certain songs. Many times you can find a master that may not be the one you wanted, but is equally as good (and well recorded). There are lots of options to explore.

**Q: What about public domain music? What about "Author Unknown"?**

A: Compositions (not masters) enter public domain (in Europe) 70 years after the death of the composer. In America, it's 50 years. If we are talking about two or more composers, it only starts counting once the last one of them dies (meaning that for the Lennon/McCartney catalog it will only start counting after Paul dies). This means that Mozart, Bach and Beethoven are already in public domain. Public domain comes from a simple and practical principle: it is reasonable that the heirs of a creator should benefit from their parents' and grand-parents' creation. However, four or five generations after the composer, we can be talking about 100 descendants. It would not be doable to be trying to obtain clearances from all of them. Public domain solves this. After that period of years after the composer's death, you can record it, you can play it, you can use it. It's public domain. However, it is not so simple. You will always need to get a master use license for Mozart's Piano Concerto, unless you own the orchestra and can produce your own master (and in that respect, there are many labels that specialize in competitively priced orchestral masters that can be licensed for a very reasonable price – just do some research and you'll find them). But most important than that, it is an illusion to think that a Mozart's piece is really free, because if you buy the sheet music and play/record it yourself on your piano, there are changes in that sheet music that have an author – so you will have to pay the publisher of the sheet music that produced the sheet music you will be using. Keep in mind that Mozart did not write his piano concertos for the pianos we have today. The same thing happens with other instruments: they have changed over the centuries, therefore, the music sheet had to go through adaptations and corrections; and regardless of if they are small or big, they were made by someone and you will be using that. However, if you play it by memory, based on the general melody instead of the precise music sheet, then you won't need to pay. The credit "Author Unknown" means that a particular song does not have a verifiable author. Certain songs, sometimes have an unknown origin (especially the very old ones). Those cases are more complex than they appear, especially if there are lyrics attached to it. Why? Because "unknown" does not mean "no author". It only means that the origin has not been investigated (are the lyrics as old as the music?). You should be very careful there, since those cases need thoroughness, because the minute you put that song in your film, all types of claims may appear.

Arrangements, simplifications, orchestrations, instrumental accompaniments, adaptations, transcriptions, translations of lyrics – all can have a copyright!


**Q: But I saw this awesome website that says the music is free.**

A: It is free under certain conditions. You must read all the fine print in order to make sure you can (a) put that music in your film and (b) make money out of your film. Most of the free stuff on the internet is free only for non-commercial uses. Once your sales agent or your distributor asks for the legal documentation, everybody realizes it's not free. You do not want to be in that position. So, read the conditions carefully. Plus: do not trust the internet. There are many sites that claim to have free content, when actually, they are just disseminating content they don't know who owns it (and don't care). The names and brands behind those sites make all the difference here. When the BBC puts something online for free under certain conditions, you can read those conditions and be sure that the BBC is the owner of that content and they can do what they are doing. The same thing with Getty Images, Adobe, the BFI, Pathé or well-known American/European content owners. What they have, they really have, and when they give it to you under certain conditions, you can trust. Other sites, beware. Remember that the internet is a labyrinth of lies just for the sake of likes and shares.

## Q: I'm not the best person to find the best solution. What should I do?

A: You hire a Music Consultant or a Music Supervisor. That person usually has encyclopedic knowledge of masters, artists, labels, publishers and musical styles. Plus, he/she has all the connections and relationships that are guaranteed to get you the best deals for your film… and he/she can and will find you a great version of Kurt Weil's "Bilbao Song" that will make perfect sense for your scene. Hiring a Music Supervisor can be a must especially if you need many songs. Producers many times do not have the time nor the knowledge to handle this issue by themselves and feel they need someone to handle such an important area. You should always consider this option.

## Q: How early should I start thinking about music?

A: There is never a too early time to start thinking about what music you will need. Considering the time it takes to negotiate and obtain the clearances you'll need and the potential disappointments that will lead you to plan B, C, D and so on, the best strategy is to start defining what you want for music still during pre-production or still during the development if possible. Better yet: try to pre-clear the songs you like and feel you'll probably will want to use. This way you'll know costs and conditions. If you already know the cost of the music you're likely to want, your budget becomes more and more credible.

## Q: What kind of music do I need?

A: Only you can answer that question. And the answer may evolve as the project itself evolves. Again, the earlier you face the issue, the best prepared you will be when the time comes to make final decisions that cannot be undone. Remember you'll have to get it right at first.

## Q: Should I go for a full orchestra or stick to a digital keyboard?

A: Both are valid options. The problem starts when the film asks for the first while your budget only allows the second. Both options don't sound the same. But depending on the project, the digital keyboard may be a great option. Or not. The key lesson here is to discuss the issue with the director and the composer observing both the film's needs and your budget possibilities. Pragmatism is the key word here. However, be careful when using cheap Digital Audio Workstations (for music creation) because sales agents and distributors who already watched too many low quality films tend to know those sounds by heart and will know immediately that you used them – and this may affect the way the market sees your film.

## Q: Can I use library music? How does it work?

A: there are several companies on the market that offer library music for a great price. There are several issues you need to reflect upon before going for such a tempting option:

1 – Library music is not tailor-made for your film. It may not be as precise as the music that was written specifically for it.
2 – Library music is not exclusive. Supposing you would find the perfect music for your film there, it is possible that the same music has been (or will be) used for selling cars, sausages, tomato sauce, vacations in Italy or worse: the music is used by another film – and a cheap, bad one! Over the time, people may watch your film feel they heard that music somewhere else. They are right.
3 – Read carefully the terms that come with the particular library music you are using. They may not include all the rights you need. Some can hide additional costs just in case you remember you need something that's not covered.
4 – When you use too much library music, the market value of your film may drop. From the sales and distribution perspective, library music is a cheap solution that does not add the value the market expects music to bring into your project. Tip: discuss this issue with a sales agent. Music is a big production value and too much library music may have a negative impact on your film. Try to listen to the feedback provided by sales people regarding your film's music.
5 – Even big, expensive Hollywood films do use library music. However, the good strategy seems the be this one: use library music in moments when the music is not particularly important or discernible. If that's the scene in question, why spend money on Queen or Bob Dylan? If it's very brief, if the volume is too low, if the setting is a noisy one or simply if you feel no one will know the difference, then library music can be the right answer.

If the library music can be modified (if the license you'll get allows you to modify it) and you are able to change it so drastically that it becomes unrecognizable and still it serves your film perfectly, then it seems you have a win-win situation. But that's easier said than done.

## Q: Are there other services that can bring music into my project?

A: Yes. There are companies that will provide music services and will even cover some (or all in some cases) of your funding needs for music they produce. They have their own composers (and many good ones, actually) and the services they provide can be very good. We will not give you names because we prefer to not do advertising here, but you can find them on the internet. This is how it works, roughly: you bring them your project and if they like it, they will let you select one of the, say, ten high-profile composers that work with them. Then he/she will write the music you need and the company will even cover the costs of recording. Music kind of stops from being a problem, since they will join your financing plan covering most costs regarding music. Sounds great? It is. However, there are a few usual catches:

1 – That music will be in your film with a limited term. In many cases, you can have it for two years. After that, you need to pay licenses renewals (both synchronization and master).
2 – You do not own nor control any of the music that's in your film (even if it was composed for it). The music is still theirs. Your film is just using it. They will monetize it afterwards how they see fit.
3 – You guessed it: the real goal of these companies is to use your film as a platform for launching their music and exploiting it after your film in any way they want. Plus, you will start paying if you want to keep the music after a certain number of years.

In a way, this type of service is several steps above the basic music libraries since the music is composed by great people, it's cheaper for you and it is much more adjusted to the musical needs of your film (although it is still debatable if the writing is really as dedicated as if you had your own composer). But it is still a service that is not entirely made to your benefit. So, it still isn't the same as having your own composer making music just for you (and having those rights). However, you should talk to them and see what they can do for you. Chances are you can negotiate a great deal or better terms. Try it!

**Q: What's the price of music? How can I get a reference of how much things cost?**

A: You can't. Although it is a big cliché, every film is unique and all music is unique. Every analysis made by a record label of if your film has what it takes to deserve a master use license is unique. It's like we said before: two nearly identical works of Art are auctioned separated by 15 minutes. The winning bid each one will reach won't be the same, since the amount paid for the first will increase or decrease the value of the second. Even if they are nearly identical. Subjectivity and intangibility are fully at play here. With music and films it's exactly the same. Precious tip: make them like your film.

**Q: Is it possible to release a soundtrack album of my film with the songs I got license for?**

A: If you are talking about the different songs whose master you are using, then the answer is "very unlikely" as record labels tend to be very conservative about letting their masters "out". Are they all coming from the same record label? If not, who will release the album? You? That's very unlikely. However, this is a discussion you can have with them. Regarding orchestral music produced by you for the film, the question is similar: who will release it and distribute it? Discuss this issue with the labels and see what they have to say about it. Making a film is complex enough. Going out of your business and producing an album adds another level of complexity.

## Q: Why should I pay for a Music Supervisor?

A: This is the answer to your question "what's the price for music?". Music Supervisors have something we, producers, don't: experience. They know who paid how much for a similar song from the same artist for a similar film six months ago. So, they know the price of licenses, musicians and all the things for which there are no written references. Practice makes perfect and they've got it. If there is a person who is best positioned to get you the best value for your dollar or euro, that's the music supervisor. Now a warning: just because the person X is a musician or used to work for a record label, that does not make him/her an automatic music supervisor. Ask around for references if you need one. Better: check recent films that had a complex list of songs and call the producer. Ask him/her about the music supervisor used in the film. Chances are those music supervisors are the ones you need.

## Q: My film has one key scene written around a specific song by Elton John.

A: When this happens, you are basically putting your entire film (the money of your investors, the hard work of amazing people and their careers – not to mention yours!) in the hands of people you don't control and couldn't care less about you. Does this seem reasonable? Are you kidding me? However, there are times when, in a script, there is one key scene that really depends on an Elton song for the entire film to click. This is the recipe for a perfect storm. But (again) in Art, many times we do have perfect storms in the making that result in full artistic and commercial triumphs.

If you feel you are about to face such situation, there are things you can do: if a certain song is that crucial to the film, it should be treated apart, with the care, urgency and respect it needs. In that case, you should dedicate an extra amount of time talking to those who control both the publishing and the master. Show them the project as it evolves, build a relationship with them. Make them love your film. Also, get a pre-clearance on that song – preferably still at script stage. Try to go as deep as possible, as early as possible and as personal as possible into guaranteeing those licenses just to make sure you won't have it exploding on your face when shooting comes and it's too late to do major changes to the script – or worse: the whole film is already shot and you never imagined you'd get a flat "no".

**Q: But Elton is my friend and he can help me.**

A: In many, many cases, this will not work. Many of those artists lost control over their publishing catalog (expensive drug habits, financial loss, creditors, divorce settlements, etc.). They may still get the royalties, but do not have a word in the pricing nor the "yes" or "no" regarding licenses (they just cry on their way to the bank). Elton John, for example, said in an interview that he sold the publishing rights of his first five albums. This means he simply cannot control them. God knows what's the case with the song you want. Paul McCartney and Yoko Ono do not control the Lennon/McCartney catalogue. Sony/ATV does. They don't control the masters either. EMI does. They just get their share of the money. That should give you an idea of how crazy this can get. Plus: if there are more writers involved and the master does not belong to your friend, he/she won't be of much help unless your amazing friend offers to reimburse you of the money you'll have to pay for licensing. We never heard of that happening.

**Q: Ok, I got the synchronization and master use licenses. Can I just start using the CD I own?**

A: If you got those licenses, you should ask who owns the master to provide you a new CD with the best/latest possible version of the song. Keep in mind that a song has many forms. There is the radio version, the single version, the clean lyrics version, the extended version, the 12'' version, the disconet version, the first CD version released in 1985 (using the vinyl master), the remastered version released on CD in 1993, the remastered version released in 2015 and so on. Chances are, the CD you gave to your post-production people is not the master you asked/paid for, nor it is the latest, nor it is the best sounding source. It is fundamental that both you and whoever is licensing the master to you, know exactly what master is being licensed to you. They must send it to you. Communication here is key.

**Q: I heard that we can use five seconds of anything for free. Or a maximum of eight notes. Or three bars. Or [insert any measure here].**

A: No.

**Q: I'm producing for television. Can I use whatever I want?**

In many countries, television channels sign agreements with collection societies that pre-clear a certain quantity of music for their use. This happens because the slow individual process of analyzing and issuing specific synchronization and master use licenses is incompatible with daily TV programming. For example, an 8 O'clock News is airing a piece tonight about an 8-year-old boy prodigy who just graduated from the Sheboygan Conservatoire, and he likes to play Elton John in his spare time.

It is obvious that the piece will show the boy playing "Goodbye Yellow Brick Road" for 10 or 15 seconds. The boy became news yesterday, the footage was recorded this morning, edited during the afternoon and aired by dinner time. Because there is no time to get those clearances and because this happens every day, TV channels make blanket agreements with collection societies where every month, the TV channel pays a fixed sum and is able to use, say, 400 songs/month from anything represented by the collection society (the exact terms of these deals vary a lot from country to country). Clearances are nearly automatic providing the channels keep track of all the songs used and send a weekly or monthly report to the collection society. There are also conditions like the impossibility using the full song (or other limitations like that). That's why TV programming is so rich in content and efficient. However, that is only possible for certain TV programs made by TV channels. They rarely cover fiction (GAME OF THRONES, THE WALKING DEAD, SEINFELD, HOUSE OF CARDS and TV movies are rarely ever covered by this type of agreement). But TV channels use these agreements extensively and this gives people the misconception that if we all only use "X" amount of seconds, we're ok. We're not. This practice (and some confusion about it) is at the origin of the previous question.

One common limitation on these agreements is that those "easy and automatic" licenses are only valid within the territory of that broadcasting. That explains why so many news videos we see on the internet are geo-locked, therefore, unavailable other countries. Even a global network like CNN cannot show 100% of its content outside the USA exactly because of the territorial limitations to those agreements.

## Q: I am licensing old 1979 archive TV footage to use on my film. There's music in that footage. What do I do?

First, the licensor of that footage should be able to tell you immediately what rights it does not have. However, this is a pretty common scenario: let's imagine that the footage in question is an interview with a famous singer that will, at some point, stand up and sing. Depending on the agreement between the artist and the network in 1979, you may need to ask for a permission from the singer (since it's his/her image, and back in 1979, he/she did not give the network an unlimited power to license his/her image beyond that program and its natural reruns). But then, there's the singing moment. If the singer is simply doing a lip-synch playback (from the record he/she was promoting in 1979), you will have to get a license both from that master and the publisher (synch). Why? Because both are "embedded" inside that 1979 TV program. Basically, you'll be re-licensing for your use the music contained inside that 1979 footage you want to use. But if the artist is singing live with his/her band (not a playback), then you can skip the master use license (since that recording belongs to the network). Occasionally, you'll find an odd scenario, where the singer is singing live (not lip-synch), but over an instrumental playback taken from the master. In this case, you'll still need to get a master use license, since (although it's just an instrumental) it's still the master from the record label. Now, if he/she sings a medley of different songs... well, you know...

:-P

But, again, the licensor should know exactly what you'll need.

## Q: I cannot find the owners of this song. How can I get a clearance for a song I can't identify?

A: This is a common question. Someone on vacation in Laos

hears a song, gets a pirated CD and no one seems to be able to identify even who's singing. The first thing we must understand is that if a song exists, it must have been written by someone. In the same vein, if a master exists, it belongs to someone. It is our job to find that person/company. Period. So, the first advice should be "don't use something you cannot clear". Once you use it without the proper licensing, you put yourself and your film into a fragile position. And the biggest the ambitions you have for your film, the more you'll have to guarantee that all the clearances exist, since the best sales agents and distributors will ask for your chain of title (where the licenses should be). Put the song on YouTube, Facebook or Twitter and ask for help and information. Go to a neighborhood where you can find people from Laos and play the song to them. Contact the Laos embassy and ask them for help – do anything (really), but make sure you can identify that song (and get the clearances). Some people will advise a different solution if you cannot identify the song:

1 – Post the song somewhere and ask for people to identify the artist.
2 – Put an ad on a newspaper with a link, ask for help identifying the song and say you want the owners of that song's rights to contact you because you want to use it in a film.
3 – Open a bank account and put in it the same average amount you paid for other songs in the film.
4 – Use the song in the film and wait for the owners to contact you.
5 – Pay them the money.

That could be a possible solution. However, you still may end up in court and even if the judge agrees that you acted reasonably and did your best effort, still, you used something that did not belong to you without permission. Only God knows what will be demanded from you. The only foolproof strategy here is this: If we can't clear a song, we'll always try to get some other song.

**Q: What about documentaries? How can I be responsible for music that comes from reality?**

A: Putting a camera somewhere means a conscious decision to record what's in front of it. Even when you cannot control what is happening in front of the camera, in reality, you can always take measures to ensure there's no Beatles playing in the background. If you are interviewing people on a mall, ask them to cut the Engelbert Humperdinck, James Last or Paul Mauriat. Better: provide them with music you already cleared and ask them to play it as you shoot. If the places where you will shoot are heavy with music, take steps to ensure the music that is played is already cleared (again, provide yourself the music). If you look hard, you'll realize that there are very few occasions when you cannot really control the music. It takes work, it's true, but it will save you some headache. Beware: some people will tell you not to bother with music in documentaries because you cannot control reality. That's silly and irresponsible. Tell it to Barry Manilow's lawyers. They will laugh at you. Don't expect to skip paying for someone else's music under the excuse that reality chose to play U2 (or anything) while you were shooting. Sony Music lawyers eat these people for breakfast. Plus, you will be damaging your film's chances later on at distribution time – because the best sales agents and distributors simply won't take the risk.

**Q: The artist I was trying to clear died and it's taking ages to get the licenses.**

A: Yes, occasionally the artist whose music you want will die. If you are lucky he/she does not control his/her publishing nor the masters, so business will go on as usual. Sometimes, when they die, it becomes a mess. We know people in Europe who were having some trouble licensing David Bowie songs in the six months after he died (and eventually the clearances arrived). Prince died without a will and people (one sister, five half-siblings and several other people) started fighting immediately. If we are lucky, his publishing catalogue and masters are safely being handled by an independent company not affected by family feuds. If we're unlucky, the fighting over his estate will affect your ability to get a clearance for years to come – one more reason to start working on those clearances early. Research!

**Q: I don't know how many minutes I will need from a song.**

A: When getting a master use license, make an estimate and then put in a little more just to be safe. If you happen to realize you used less than that, then try to ask for a reduction on the price asked, since, well, you ended up using less. It's not guaranteed to work, but you should try.

**Q: How many options I should consider for music?**

A: When you start development, make a list of the music you imagine in the film. Now go do your research and see how much they cost. Found something scary? The good news is that you are still in development and you should be able to budget your music in a way that is realistic and it fulfills the film's needs. From then on, keep an eye on the evolution of the project and its impact on your music budget. For every song you think you want, make sure you have alternatives that are adequate for the film, available and cheaper. Due to the fact that you do not control other people's music, always have a plan B, C, D and E.

**Q: My director put Led Zeppelin as temp music and it's perfect. What should I do?**

A: Temporary music has this problem: we use it freely because we know it's temp. But as we use it (sometimes for months), we begin to love the way it suits the project. Yes, the director and the editors did walk into a trap they created. Now they can only imagine Led Zeppelin on the scene and nothing else works! There is no easy solution for this problem. They have to understand that temp music was just temp music and now it comes a time get the music that is possible (unless you have the unlimited funds and personal connections that would allow you to get Led Zeppelin). It will hurt, but they must realize the trap if they expect to free themselves and finish the film.

**Q: Why are sales agents and distributors so picky about music rights?**

A: A film costs a lot of money. Distributing a film also costs a lot of money. No distributor and no sales agent will touch your film if there is any hint that there are issues with rights (regarding music or anything).

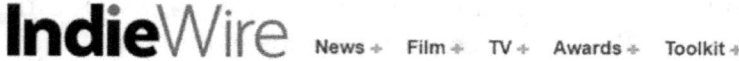

**IndieWire** News + Film + TV + Awards + Toolkit +

## 'Baby Driver's Soundtrack Leads to a Lawsuit Over Inclusion of T. Rex Song 'Debora'

Ansel Elgort may have to make one last getaway drive.

If this happens in Hollywood (who has the money muscle to hire the best clearance people), it can happen anywhere.

No one wants to set a release date, spend money in promotion only to receive a court order freezing everything because a contract is missing or a master use license is missing. Even in cases where you end up being right, no one wants to find that out after a long legal battle. You should have all the needed licenses in your chain of title as soon as possible. Sometimes even big Hollywood films have problems – and those are the guys who have all the legal muscle that should prevent problems from happening. THE HANGOVER, PART II had a problem regarding the reproduction of the tattoo design on Mike Tyson's face. Who the hell would have thought of that? Be careful.

**Q: I cleared the music for the film. Can I use it also on the trailer?**

A: No. A trailer is a trailer; a film is a film. By obtaining the clearances for a song to appear on your film, the clearances are just for the film. Putting the song in a trailer means to do the process all over again. Bear in mind that it will probably cost you more than it cost for the film, since the trailer will be seen by a potentially much larger crowd. If a trailer contains a portion of the scene with the song in case, your trailer editors will have to take the song out and find a clever way to make it work without the song (luckily, trailers have their own music). The lesson here is simple: every teaser, every trailer, every making of is – when it comes to clearing music rights – a different film.

**Q: How can I make sure all rights and licenses with my film are ok?**

A: You can hire a consultant to check your Chain of Title or you can take an Insurance of Errors & Omissions (E&O). Consider using E&O insurance to manage risk of liability. This is a special form of liability insurance that is used to insure against claims that may appear later: in the promotion, distribution and exhibition of your film. E&O policies typically provide coverage for claims in the nature of invasion of privacy, defamation, publicity, copyright (here we are!) and trademark infringement, wrongful portrayal, piracy, plagiarism, or unfair competition resulting from the alleged unauthorized use of titles, formats, ideas, characters, plots, performances of artists or performers or other material. The E&O lawyers will take a look at the whole film and verify if all the legal documentation is in order. By buying an E&O your film is guaranteed to be ok for any sales agent or distributor. From that point on, should anything happen regarding rights (something that even the E&O people missed), you are covered. □

## Q: Is it harder for horror films to get good music?

A: It shouldn't be (and the upcoming case studies will show you that). However, some rights owners are extra careful regarding the nature and context where their music will be featured. Extreme violence, gore and sex sometimes can be a problem when you are talking to, say, a Disney (for obvious reasons). But there are good news. Some genres (Death Metal comes to mind, but there are others) are not very popular with mainstream films and TV and will be very open to participate in a horror film. Actually, many of those musicians are hardcore horror fans and will be thrilled to license you their music and will make great prices.

## Q: I want to use a song in my film, but I've noticed it contains a sample from another song/master. How do I deal with it?

A: Sampling is the new normal in contemporary music. However, it raises a few questions when it comes to licensing for films and TV. Modjo has a song called "Lady (Hear Me Tonight)", written by Yann Destagnol and Romain Tranchart, that contains a sample from Chic's "Soup for One" written by Nile Rodgers and Bernard Edwards. This sample is now part of the master owned by Modjo. In case you want to use "Lady (Hear Me Tonight)" in your film, when obtaining the master use license, try to understand what were the conditions under which the sample from Chic's "Soup for One" ended in Modjo's master. Can Modjo license its master (containing a sample from another master and a different song from a different publisher) freely? When Modjo licensed the sample for inclusion in their song and master, did that license come with any limitations to what Modjo could do with the subsequent master? Keep in mind that the licensing of a sample (to an artist who wants to incorporate that sample into a new song) is a process that is similar to licensing that song for a film. Modjo needed the license from Chic's publisher (for the song) and Chic's record label (for the master use) – that's how the sample ended in their song. For Modjo (or any artist who want to use a sample), costs of licensing a sample vary a lot. As a rule of thumb, the more popular, recognizable and longer the sample, the costlier it will be. The artist who wants the sample can be charged a flat fee or a rolling fee payable every certain milestones. For example: $200.00 upon getting the clearance, $600.00 if the song gets picked up by a major U.S. label and $1500.00 for every 100,000 units sold. The copyright owner may want to get a royalty in perpetuity for other licensing, like in the case a producer (you) wants Modjo's song in a film.

You have to make sure that by getting the clearance from Modjo (who controls their song's publishing and master) you are not infringing the samples' owners' copyrights. It may sound overzealous to start from the song you want and look deeper into the whole sample licensing obligations, however, again, it is your film that may be blocked from distribution by a furious artist until everything gets sorted out. Plus, the current music scene is filled with a gazillion cases of sample issues.

Remember Danger Mouse's "Grey Album"? So, ask the artists

what are the situations, obligations and limitations of the samples they licensed for use in their songs and always try to get straight answers. Of course, reputable artists, when using samples from other works tend to be careful. It's hard to imagine Beyoncé or Madonna being caught in sampling issues. However, one never knows the potential problems regarding samples used by big or small artists. History is filled with big names in trouble: Vanilla Ice, MC Hammer and The Verve are just a few names that come to mind.

A slightly different scenario is the incorporation of a song inside another song (without the use of a master): yes, occasionally you will find songs where writers sample other songs resulting in new compositions. They mixed their own lyrics with a pre-existing one. Finley Quaye recorded "Sunday Shining" for his 1997 album "Maverick A Strike". However, the song, written by Quaye incorporates several samples (portions) of Bob Marley's classic song "Sun Is Shining" (written by Bob Marley). The credits of the 1997 song state Quaye/Marley and the publishing is split between both writers. Using Quaye's song in your film means getting a clearance from both publishers – just as the credits suggest. Again, you should proceed with caution.

In 2007, Rihanna sampled Michael Jackson's "Wanna Be Startin' Somethin'" (from the legendary album "Thriller", 1982) for her hit single "Don't Stop the Music". After the song's release, she and Michael Jackson were sued by Camaroonian musician Manu Dibango, who claimed that the line "mama-say mama-sa mama-coo-sa" was taken from his 1972 single "Soul Makossa" without permission. Although Jackson admitted that he borrowed the hook for his song and settled out of court, Rihanna was inevitably dragged along for using the line without permission (from the right owner). Rihanna asked the sample to Jackson not knowing the line did not belong to him originally (or if she knew, she thought Jackson had it covered). He didn't. When asked for the permission to be sampled, Jackson allowed it without asking for the approval from Dibango. Although a film that had licensed "Don't Stop the Music" would probably not be impacted by the case, a film producer may find him/herself

being targeted in a similar case (especially if the film makes money or its profile grows). Angry rights holders will try to get the money where the money is – or they think it is.

All the examples above suggest that film producers must be careful and dedicate extra time to fully understand the nature and origin of the songs they are trying to license.


**Q: Do I also have to pay for translations of songs?**

A: Most of the times, yes. If you want to use in your film "The Girl from Ipanema", you must obtain the clearance from an additional writer: Norman Gimbel (the writer of the lyrics of "Killing Me Softly with His Song") who wrote the English version from a translation of the Portuguese version. But using the English version does not mean you can skip paying the Brazilian writer (for the original lyrics). You will still have to get the clearance from Antônio Carlos Jobim's (music) and Vinícius de Moraes' (lyrics) publishers. Why? Because the English translation (even if it's not literal) comes from the Portuguese version.

In a slightly different way, "My Way" (immortalized by Frank Sinatra) is the completely original English language lyrics written by Paul Anka from the French song "Comme d'Habitude", written by Claude François and Jacques Revaux with lyrics by Claude François and Gilles Thibaut. Anka bought the publishing rights to the French song and scraped the French lyrics entirely (he negotiated that way). If you want to use Anka's version, you'll pay Anka, François and Revaux (no payment to the French lyrics writers, since the English version has no connection to it). If you want to use the French version, there are two versions of it with different lyrics. You'll have to select one and get the clearance from the respective writers (minus Paul Anka, of course). Now, the masters are a different story: each version is a different one.

From these examples, it should be clear that every song is a world in itself.

## Q: When working with composers, should the producer keep the control over the publishing and master?

A: Whenever possible, yes. Music is an integral part of your film. Whatever is done with that music can have an impact on your film. So, from the producer's point of view, he/she has to protect both the film and its original music soundtrack. If the producer does not have control over what can be done with the music, he/she may face unforeseeable issues later on. Because of the multiple dimensions of a film, a producer many times is in a better position to promote and protect the film's soundtrack than the composer is. Keep in mind that the full original music soundtrack (and not just the portions that were used in the film) is a normal item on the deliverables list the producer has to fulfill to the sales agent. Why? Because one distributor in France will want to do radio spots to promote the film and needs access to all the music (or cues) in order to select what works best. Another distributor in Argentina needs to cut a new trailer and needs the same access to the whole music. This means that there are lots of possible music uses (some are not that obvious) that will always depend on what the producer can allow or control. Composers should not be bothered with this. As time goes, if the music is that memorable, it's usage still can impact the film. With that in mind, the producer (and/or the sales agent) usually has the back-office muscle to keep track of all that's going on regarding music usage and protect the composer's rights. The bigger your ambitions are for your film, the more complex the managing of the music tends to be as sales and promotion go. You should not leave that flux of responsibility to the composer. You should always look at the Laws in your country, and see specific limitations to who can own or control the publishing, since there are some variations here. Also, it is advisable to respect guild and union rules (on the producing country) regarding the composer's share and eventual residuals.

## Q: Can I mention titles of songs in my script?

A: Yes. Mentioning things and people is not a problem. In the beginning of RESERVOIR DOGS (1992) the characters discuss the meaning of Madonna's "Like a Virgin". There is no problem there. The problem only starts if a character sings a passage from the song (melody) or quotes the lyrics. In that case, if you want to avoid potential trouble, you should get a license or ask for a permission from the rights holders.

## Q: My art department wants some classic album covers on the walls of the set. What do I do?

A: Album covers and all graphic content that comes with an album are protected too. Think about Joy Division's "Unknown Pleasures", The Police's "Ghost in the Machine" or Debbie Harry's "Koo Koo". You will have to obtain a permission (and likely pay) from either the record label (that owns or controls the "album" as a whole), the Graphic Artist who created that Art, or both! It all depends on the contractual powers and obligations between who owns the album and the Graphic Artist. Also, you will be facing the same issue if those Artworks appear on the t-shirt your character is wearing on scene 53. This can be quite a problem, since, in the last 20 years, virtually every classic album Artwork has been licensed for merchandising – so much, we don't even notice it anymore.

How do you defend yourself? Tell your Art department to not use any protected I.P. on the film. Better yet: ask your Art department to create fake record covers (and these you control). It's okay to write made-up band names over a fake cover. It's equally ok to slightly alter a band's name and create a similar logo (never use their original logos, since they too are protected) if you think the audience won't notice, or if they still will make the connection. The Police's album "Ghost in the Machine" goes to the extra length of writing that the digital gibberish of the cover artwork is trademarked – so you cannot use it! However, you can produce yourself something similar and let the audience make the connection.

**Q: I know two singers whose voices sound just like Tom Waits and Bette Midler. Can I use them to make it look like I licensed their songs?**

A: Be very careful there. We are not citing Waits and Midler just because. Earlier we discussed the use of sound-alikes. However, there are limits to what you can accomplish with sound-alikes. If you want Adele to sing in your film but cannot get the real deal, you can hire one of the many sound-alikes available in the market. But be careful to NOT make them sing a song from the original artist (Adele). Why? Because if you do, the original Artist can take you to court for misleading the audience into thinking they did sing on your film or licensed their masters. Bette Midler and Tom Waits are two great examples. Better said: Midler Vs. Ford Motor Co. and Waits Vs. Frito Lay are two great examples. In the 80's, Ford wanted to use Bette Midler on a commercial. When she declined, they licensed her 1972 hit song "Do You Wanna Dance?" (written by Bobby Freeman) from the publisher and hired a sound-alike to sing it. Midler took them to court and won. The same happened with Waits, who is well-known for refusing any connection with Advertising. Frito-Lay wanted to use Tom Waits' "Step Right Up" from his 1976 album "Small Change" on a commercial. Although the song was written by Waits, he does not control the publishing. The record label does. Frito-Lay licensed it from the record label and hired Stephen Carter, who was known as an impersonator of Tom Waits, having performed his songs in the past. His version of "Step Right Up" was so perfect even Tom Waits was amazed (or too amazed). So, he took Frito-Lay to court and won over 2 million dollars in damages because the snacks company misled the audience into thinking that was Tom Waits backtracking in his disdain for advertising. So, the lesson here is simple: if you want to have Adele, Amy Winehouse, Tom Waits, Freddie Mercury or any distinct Artist – but cannot have him/her for some reason – do not use a sound-alike to "reproduce" a classic master. Instead, use the sound-alike to sing something else in the style of the said Artist.

## Q: Are there legal exceptions to anything in this guide?

A: Yes. There may be exceptions to anything in this guide. Those exceptions will come from the rights owner's power over what he/she owns or from specificities in different countries' legislation. A country may allow you to do one thing or another differently. However, you should keep in mind that those exceptions and differences only apply in that country. So, if Luxembourg law allows you to include music in your film without any licensing (not true, by the way), that will only be valid when your film is distributed in Luxembourg. An artist may love your project and give his/her music for free providing you give him/her a foot massage. You are in the entertainment business: anything can happen! However, be careful and always think strategically. Understand that your film will be released some day and music licensing is a delicate business.

In the next section we selected some well-known films and tried to explain some elements on the music they licensed. We picked those titles not just because we love them (we do), but also because they offer a wide variety of approaches. With those titles, we cover over 35 years of filmmaking. Very little has changed from the music rights' perspective.

## 7 – THE CONJURING 2 (2016)

THE CONJURING 2 presents a great case study, since it contains a good number of songs that help tell the story and create all the elements the film needs.

The original music score (non-diegetic) was composed by Joseph Bishara, who is totally at ease with the horror genre. He is the music composer for several horror films that got theatrical distribution worldwide – including INSIDIOUS (2010), GRACE (2014), THE VATICAN TAPES (2015) and of course THE CONJURING (2013) and its spin-off ANNABELLE (2014).

Music supervisor is Dana Sano (LEE DANIEL'S THE BUTLER (2013), THE CABIN IN THE WOODS (2012) and FRIGHT NIGHT (2011)).

Music clearances by Jessica Dolinger (TUSK (2014), CARRIE (2013), FREDDY VS. JASON (2003))

Below, we are reproducing the music credits both as an example of how to do proper music credits and to show the amount of songs that need licensing – people usually don't sit and count the songs that appear in the rolling credits.

The story is set in the seventies, so expect a lot of flavor of that decade coming through music.

"LONDON CALLING"
Written by Strummer and Jones
Performed by The Clash
Courtesy of Sony Music Entertainment (UK) Ltd.
by Arrangement with Sony Music Licensing

The song is brilliantly used to set the location and time of the story. As the story starts with the two main characters in the USA, the moving of the story to London, UK needs a song that clearly tells the audience where we are now.

"BUS STOP"
Written by Graham Gouldman
Performed by The Hollies
Courtesy of Parlophone Records Ltd.
by Arrangement with Warner Music Group Film & TV Licensing

In a similar manner, this song communicates the life of school kids in 1970's London. The music is played as the kids come home from school.

These two choices are an example of well-known songs that have the power to instantly transport the audience to a particular place and time, while also infusing the scenes with some insights about how those characters behave, their social class, their relationships and their innocence.

"THERE WAS A CROOKED MAN"
Written by Joseph Bishara

The song that is played by the toy associated with a monster.

"THIS OLD MAN"
Traditional
Arranged and Performed by Ben Parry

This old nursery rhyme is whistled during a scary scene.
Although it's a traditional song, Ben Parry wrote and
performed the version used.

"BORED TEENAGERS"
Written by TV Smith
Performed by The Adverts
Courtesy of Fire Records

This song is heard for less than one second as Janet changes the
TV channels.

"THE FIRST NOEL"
Traditional
Performed by Slovak State Philharmonic Orchestra
Courtesy of Naxos
by Arrangement with Source Q

Although this song is a traditional composition with no
attributable writer, the recording is provided by Naxos (owner
of the master) that is represented by Source Q (a licensing
company that represents several labels).

## "CAN'T HELP FALLING IN LOVE"
Written by Luigi Creatore, George Davis Weiss
and Hugo E. Peretti
Performed by Elvis Presley
Courtesy of RCA Records
by Arrangement with Sony Music Licensing

This song appears two times in the film: once sung by actor
Patrick Wilson and later the Elvis Presley version. Two times
mean two licenses.

## "JOLLY CHRISTMAS MEDLEY"
Arranged by Robert J. Walsh and James E. Moore
Performed by Robert J. Walsh
Courtesy of Chicago Music Library

This song is a good example of library music usage. There is no
particular need for a certain version of Christmas song. Robert
J. Walsh is an experienced composer associated music libraries.

## "I STARTED A JOKE"
Written by Barry Gibb, Robin Gibb and Maurice Gibb
Performed by The Bee Gees
Courtesy of Rhino Entertainment Company
by Arrangement with Warner Music Group Film and TV
Licensing

This classic song by The Bee Gees sets the sad tone when it
seems the haunting was a hoax.

## "DON'T GIVE UP ON US"
Written by Tony MacAulay
Performed by David Soul
Courtesy of Topanga Music
by Arrangement with Ace Music Services LLC.

Margaret is listening to this song, a big hit in 1977.

"DON'T WORRY TRACY"
Written by Doug Davis
Performed by Christopher Blue
Courtesy of Fervor Records

This is the example of a record label that controls the master and the publishing of the song.

"PHOTOGRAPH" and "HAPPY FAMILY"
from THE CONJURING
Composed by Mark Isham

These songs come from the first film.

Elvis Presley TM; Rights of Publicity and Persona Rights:
Elvis Presley Enterprises, LLC. Elvis.com
"Blue Hawaii" album cover courtesy of
Sony Music Entertainment

Both the Elvis persona and the artwork regarding his films need rights clearance.

Corbis

Corbis is a rights licensing company.

Taking a look at the music credits in THE CONJURING 2 it is possible to see how varied it gets. The film contains classic pop songs, lesser known pop songs, library music, a medley, traditional songs and even returning songs from a previous film. Plus, some songs appear more than once onscreen and one of them is sung by the actor. The structure of licensing is also quite diverse. There are cases where publishing and master are controlled by different entities, songs where both are controlled by the same entity and even a case where the producer of the film controls master and publishing.

PAULO LEITE

## 8 – IT FOLLOWS (2014)

With a budget that is a fraction of the previous case study, IT FOLLOWS (2014) has a careful strategy of relying on music with a simplified licensing – independent music from independent artists that control both their masters and publishing.

The main credit for music is:

Music by Disasterpeace

However, the song list is as follows:

"WEAPONS OF VELVET"
Written and Performed by Dan Cantrell
Courtesy of Dan Cantrell

"THE SAFER PARTS OF THE CITY"
Written by Steven Slovacek
Performed by Company Man
Courtesy of Dugout Sounds

"WALTER, YOU'VE BEEN WARNED"
Written by Steven Slovacek
Performed by Company Man
Courtesy of Dugout Sounds

"EXOTATING"
Written by Franklin Randall Hare and & Loren A. Robinson
Performed by Metal Sky Craz
Courtesy of Franklin Randall Hare

Commercial Footage Courtesy of Father & Son Construction,
Used By Permission
Additional Footage Courtesy of eFootage, LLC,
Used By Permission
Stock Media Provided by Cinematologist / Pond5.com

While the non-diegetic orchestral score (by Disasterpeace) of mostly electronic music contributes a lot to emphasizing and reinforcing the key dramatic elements and moments of the story, the songs do not seem to be particularly relevant to the story. However, as they play in the background, what they do is to reflect the teenage characters' tastes in current independent music – in a way, helping characterization. Contrary to THE CONJURING 2, they do not try to establish a year or a decade. The story takes place here and now. Contrary to I AM LEGEND (2007), there are no onscreen discussions about an artist that calls for the use of his/her songs. With that in mind, it's safe to say that the script wisely avoids music that is either too expensive or hard to obtain. It is not that the song choice is unimportant. Its just that the film allows the producers to have many good and affordable options. The two songs by Steven Slovacek come from the same album by Company Man, "The Headless" (and the song "Walter, You've Been Warned" appears in another film, THE MYTH OF THE AMERICAN SLEEPOVER (2011)). The other songs seem to be entirely controlled by one person. A great approach.

## 9 – EVIL DEAD (2013)

EVIL DEAD (2013) is completely different from THE CONJURING 2 and IT FOLLOWS. The nature of the film demands mostly a non-diegetic score.

Music Composed, Conducted
& Orchestrated by Roque Baños.

Music Editor Maarten Hofmeijer.

Scoring Production, Additional Orchestration
& Music Preparation Coordinator Ginés Carrión.

Music Preparation Kira Moreno Morales.

Lyricist Juan Miguel Valero.

Additional Music Programming by Felix Erskine.

Score Recorded and Mixed at
Air Lyndhurst Studios
London, England

with the
Pro Arte Orchestra and the BTG Chapel Choir

The music of EVIL DEAD creates the sound atmosphere for
the great violence and shocks the audience expects from a
remake of the 1981 horror classic we all love. With that in
mind, be ready for a complex and multi-layered music that
takes everything an orchestra and a choir can give. There are no
radios, parties, TV sets or anything that will ask for music. The
film will not let go of its essence: young, possessed people
locked in an old cabin killing each other in the most gruesome
way – exactly what we want!

"BABY, LITTLE BABY"
Written by Fede Alvarez and Rodo Sayagues
Performed by Jane Levy and Shiloh Fernandez
Published by Fede Alvarez (ASCAP) and Rodo Sayagues
(ASCAP)

The character Mia sings this song in a specific moment of the
film. Instead of paying for the clearance of a pre-existing song
or going for a traditional lullaby, director Fede Alvarez and
Writer Rodo Sayagues decided to write the lullaby themselves.
Of course, although they do not control the master (because it
was recorded as part of the film) they do control the publishing.
Depending on the film's evolving profile (will it become a cult
film or a classic?), chances are someone will want to cover the
song. That means money.

## 10 – I AM LEGEND (2007)

I AM LEGEND (2007) is a big Hollywood film, so they can afford some memorable songs and other high profile intellectual properties.

"THREE LITTLE BIRDS"
Written by Bob Marley
Performed by Bob Marley and The Wailers
Courtesy of The Island Def Jam Music Group
Under License from Universal Music Enterprises

This song (played twice in the film plus a third time sung by the main character) is a great counterpoint to what's happening around Robert Neville as his mind jumps between past and present while bathing the dog. They could have used a cheaper, less-known song. But this one is iconic and brings to our minds the opposite of Robert's reality. The contrast between past and present is, thus, clearly established.

"FLYING TALKING DONKEY" from SHREK
Written by Harry Gregson-Williams and John Powell
Courtesy of Dreamworks Animation L.L.C.

This part from SHREK (2001) is recited by Robert Neville as the film plays. This is treated the same way as if this was a song sung by the character.

"I SHOT THE SHERIFF"
Written by Bob Marley

A verse of the song is sung by the main character.

"STIR IT UP"
Written by Bob Marley
Performed by Bob Marley and The Wailers
Courtesy of The Island Def Jam Music Group
Under License from Universal Music Enterprises

This song is played as Robert Neville talks about Bob Marley.

"REDEMPTION SONG"
Written by Bob Marley
Performed by Bob Marley and The Wailers
Courtesy of The Island Def Jam Music Group
Under License from Universal Music Enterprises

This song is played over the end credits.

CORBIS
The NYPD and FDNY name, logos and insígnia are trademarks
of The City of New York and are used
with the City's permission.
"Green Lantern"™, "Teen Titans"™ & © DC Comics
All Rights Reserved. Used with permission.
"Shrek"® & © 2001 DreamWorks Animation LLC,
Used with Permission of DreamWorks Animation LLC
NBC News Archives
Keith Haring Artwork © The Estate of Keith Haring.
Used with Permission

These rights also had to be cleared by the film's producers. However, it is interesting that other brands like "Batman", "Superman" and "Time" also appear in the film. Why aren't they mentioned here? Probably because I AM LEGEND is a Warner film, and Warner Bros already controls these licenses. Inside a cabinet, one can also see a DVD copy of GOODFELLAS (1990), another Warner movie.

## 11 – HOSTEL (2005)

HOSTEL (2005) has a long list of songs that comes from the fact that the film contains many scenes of parties, clubs and situations that need diegetic music. Those songs and the non-diegetic orchestral score are concentrated in different parts of the film. On the first 20 minutes, diegetic music dominates due to the frequent party scenes. However, after the group arrives in Slovakia, the music changes. At first, the non-diegetic music starts to paint the hostel as an idyllic spa filled with gorgeous women. Then it starts to rapidly change tone as the horror becomes more present and real. The songs played in the parties turn to Slovakian pop and rock songs. As the violence becomes more and more grotesque, non-diegetic music kicks in with all the sound elements we expect in a horror film. The main music credits are:

Music by Nathan Barr

FILMharmonic Orchestra Prague

Music Supervision by Gerry Cueller and Greg Danylynshyn

Music Supervision, Czech Republic, by Tomas Belohradsky

It is worth noting that Nathan Barr worked in Eli Roth's previous feature, CABIN FEVER (2002). Gerry Cueller and Greg Danylynshyn are a team of music supervisors who work together in many films and TV series. The film also needs an additional music supervisor from the Czech Republic to deal with the local songs that the film needs.

"THE SURGEON"
Written by Eli Roth

This theme was composed by the director himself, similar to what we saw in EVIL DEAD. It is absent from the film's soundtrack record that contains only Nathan Barr's work. Sometimes directors like to write a specific theme they want the film to have either for purely creative reasons (they already had that music in their minds long before the composer started working on the film's music) or for purely commercial reasons (they want to be the ones who control a theme they think will become a classic tune and/or appear in sequels as well as other films). This theme appears in HOSTEL Part II (2007).

"5 SECONDS"
Written by Ryan Sollum, Kyle Klima, Justin Halladay, Matt Ferro & Jor Bol
Performed by Shortie
Courtesy of Hard 2 Pronounce Music, LLC

This song starts the story as the characters hit the streets of Amsterdam.

"ODDITY"
Written by Danny Doyal
Performed by The Phonosapiens
Courtesy of 750mph Music, LLC

"MASSACRE"
Written by Paul Cafaro
Performed by The Dwarves
Courtesy of Greedy / Sympathy for the Record Industry

This song plays as the character Josh (in the Amsterdam sequence) walks along a corridor where prostitutes and clientes can be seen as shadows on the doors. This song also appears in another film: DIRTY (2005).

HOSTEL takes another very efficient approach: no need for well-known American songs. Instead, the film goes for independent music, public domain songs and old Czech or Slovak pop songs as it characterizes that zone of the globe as old, backwards and underdeveloped.

"SOME KINDA FREAK"
Written by Orpheus Djournette & Mikael Johnston
Performed by Mephisto Odyssey
Courtesy of Warner Bros. Records, Inc.
by Arrangement with Warner Music Group Film & TV Licensing

This song plays at the club, where the characters get thrown out because of a fight.

"WE AIN'T FUCKIN' WIT Y'ALL"
Written by Shawn Thomas
Performed by C-BO
Courtesy of West Coast Mafia Records

"PRAVDA VITAZI"
Written by Martin Durinda & Martin Sarvas
Performed by Tublatanka
Courtesy of Opus Records

This song is a Slovak rock song that is played at the club where the three characters party with the two girls they just met. In this scene guys try drugs and a Chinese female character is introduced.

"TRETI GALAXIE"
Written by Giancarlo Bigazzi, Umberto Tozzi and Michael Prostejovsky
Performed by Michal David and Kroky Frantiska Janecka
Courtesy of Supraphon

This Czech pop song plays as the two main characters try to party while worried about Oli.

"DRZIM TI MIESTO"
Written by Julius Kincek and Daniel Hevier
Performed by Team
Courtesy of Opus Records

"DARK EYES"
Traditional

As the character Oli learns at the spa that one of the girls has a Russian father, he starts singing this traditional song in its Russian version. The Russian version from the 19th Century with its original Russian lyrics is public domain – unlike other later versions and translations (including one in English) that are not yet in public domain.

"DARK EYES"
Written by Dimitri Oleg Yachino
Performed by National Tatarstan Orchestra & Choir
Courtesy of Lovecat Music
by Arrangement with Ocean Park Music Group

This song should not be confused with the traditional Ukranian traditional song in public domain.

"GUTEN ABEND"
Written by Johannes Brahms

Public domain.

"V SLEPYCH ULICKACH"
Written by Meky Zbirka and Kamil Peteraj
Performed by Meky Zbirka and Marika Gombitova
Courtesy of Opus Records

This song plays at the club, when Josh talks to the Dutch businessman. It plays again later, when Paxton finds the girls in a bar.

"STUZKOVA"
Written by Jozo Raz and Boris Filan
Performed by Elan
Courtesy of MC Production s.r.o.

"PULP FICTION"
C 1994 Miramax Films
Courtesy of Quentin Tarantino and Miramax Films

This clip from PULP FICTION (1994) plays with a comic Czech dubbing as the characters check into the hostel. It is important to note that beyond licensing a clip from the producer (Miramax Films), the producers had to either license the original Czech dubbing actor or pay someone to do a new version of the Czech language dub. Here, it all depends on the price and the comic effect needed.

## "HOW DO"
Written by Anthony Christopher Corner, Coverdale Liam Howe & Richard Ian Pickering
Performed by The Sneaker Pimps
Courtesy of Virgin Records and One Little Indian Records
Under License from EMI Film & Television Music and One Little Indian Ltd.

This song plays as the main characters have sex in the Hostel with the two girls they just met. It contains portions of "Willow's Song" (by Paul Giovanni) from the British classic THE WICKER MAN (1973). The whole narrative context is also very similar as the characters are being seduced to be sacrificed. The homage is totally justified.

## "SEX FEVER"
© 2003 L.F.P. Productions
Courtesy of L.F.P. Productions

## "CHODNIK CEZ DUNAJ"
© 1989 Miroslav Luther
Courtesy of Film Archive of the Slovakian Film Institute, Bratislava

## 12 – SCREAM (1996)

The music soundtrack of SCREAM is an effective blend of large orchestral and electronic non-diegetic music and diegetic songs. The music makes every effort to create the right mood or simply to enhance the horror scenes. Its use of female voices evokes some classic horror soundtracks of the past. It all works beautifully. The music credits are:

Music by Marco Beltrami
Music Supervisor Jeffrey Rabhan
Background Vocals Rose Thomson
Orchestra Conducted by Marco Beltrami
Orchestrations by Peter Anthony and William A. Boston
Music Consultant Ed Gerrard

"DON'T FEAR THE REAPER"
Performed by Gus
Written by Donald Roeser
Courtesy of Sony/ATV Tunes LLC

This song is played as Sidney and Billy make out on her bed. She breaks it and they say goodbye.

"WHISPER"
Performed by Catherine
Written by Keith Brown, Kerry Brown and Mark Rew
Courtesy of TVT Records

This song is played as the characters sit next to a fountain discussing the murders.

"ARTIFICIAL WORLD" (INTERDIMENSIONAL MIX)
Performed by Julee Cruise With The Flow
Written by Julee Cruise, Louis Tucci, Supa D.J. Dmitry and D.J. Silver

This song plays at Tatum's room. Tatum is excited about Sidney punching Gale.

"RED RIGHT HAND"
Performed by Nick Cave & The Bad Seeds
Written by Nick Cave, Mick Harvey and Thomas Wydler
Courtesy of Mute Records Limited U.K.
by Arrangement with Warner Special Products

This song plays twice in the film. First, briefly as Sidney sees her attack on the News. Later, a longer portion with Nick Cave's lyrics as the city prepares for curfew. The two moments use different parts of the song. The first uses an instrumental solo while the second uses the main lyrics. That way, the same song looks like two different songs.

"BETTER THAN ME"
Performed by Sister Machine Gun
Written by Chris Randall
Courtesy of Wax Trax! Records/TVT Records

This song plays when the characters meet after the announcement that classes are suspended and a curfew has been issued.

"SCHOOL'S OUT"
Performed by Alice Cooper
Written by Alice Cooper and Michael Bruce
Courtesy of Warner Bros. Records
by Arrangement with Warner Special Products

This song plays as Sidney and Tatum talk on the porch after the principal is murdered. This classic song has appeared in dozens of films before and after SCREAM – most notably, ROCK'N'ROLL HIGH SCHOOL (1979), THE SIMPSONS (1992), DAZED AND CONFUSED (1993), REALITY BITES (1994) and GLEE (2012).

"YOUTH OF AMERICA"
Performed by Birdbrain
Written by Ammo
Courtesy of TVT Records

This song plays as the characters drive to the party while Gale Weathers follows them in TV News van.

"BITTER PILL"
Performed by The Connells
Written by Peele Wimberley
Courtesy of TVT Records

This song plays Billy appears at the door. Sidney takes him upstairs.

"DROP DEAD GORGEOUS"
Performed by Republica
Written by Republica
Courtesy of RCA U.K. Ltd./Deconstruction Records

This song plays as Deputy Dewey enters the party with Gale Weathers who plants a hidden camera in the living room. Tatum gets locked in the garage. The song continues after Tatum's murder as the killer opens the door and goes back into the house.

"FIRST COOL HIVE"
Performed by Moby
Written by Richard Hall Group/Mute Records Limited U.K.

This song plays as the police takes the survivors and Gale starts narrating the events for her TV show.

"WHISPER TO A SCREAM"
Performed by Soho
Written by Robert Ian McNabb
Administered by Chappel & Co.

This song is the first one to play over the end credits.

"I DON'T CARE"
Performed by Dillon Dixon, Marco Beltrami and Steve Carnelli
Written by Marco Beltrami

This song is the third one played over the end credits. Between this and the first song played, there is a brief musical passage with atmospheric original music.

Rose Thomson Appears Courtesy of the RCA Records Label

Rose Thomson does voice work is some of the musical passages.

Soundtrack Available on TVT Records

TVT Records controls four of the 12 masters on this list.

HALLOWEEN Footage courtesy of
Compass International Pictures

Several clips from the film are used during the party. The film
is also constantly mentioned and discussed by the characters.

FRANKENSTEIN Footage courtesy of MCA/Universal

A clip from this film is shown at the video rental store.

Ghost Mask courtesy of
Funworld Division of Easter Unlimited, Inc.

The mask used in the film (and later in the franchise) is
copyrighted. The film uses it under a license. It is interesting to
note that the producers of the TV series decided to create their
own mask, owning the licensing themselves.

Looking at the songs list, one does not find artists that have a
special connection with the horror genre – which is kind of odd
considering the film's reflexive nature as it constantly
comments upon the genre it belongs to. The only notable
exception is Alice Cooper, who has, over the years, been a
constant presence in horror films soundtracks like MONSTER
DOG (1984), JASON LIVES: FRIDAY THE 13TH PART VI
(1996), PRINCE OF DARKNESS (1987) and more recently,
HALLOWEEN (2007).

## 13 – FROM DUSK TILL DAWN (1996)

FROM DUSK TILL DAWN is a good case study as an example of a song list that repeats several artists: three songs by Tito & Tarantula, Two songs by ZZ Top, two songs by Jimmie Vaughan and two songs by Stevie Ray Vaughan. The band Tito & Tarantula appears onscreen as they lip-synch their songs and get a credit with the cast – similar to what happened to Bauhaus in THE HUNGER (1983) and many other bands.

The film's main music credits are:

Music by Graeme Revell
Music Consultants Mary Ramos and Chuck Kelley
Music Orchestrated and Conducted by Tim Simonec

Graeme Revell is no stranger to horror. He wrote the music for DEAD CALM (1989), CHILD'S PLAY 2 (1990), PSYCHO IV THE BEGINNING (1990) and GHOST IN THE MACHINE (1993). After FROM DUSK TILL DAWN, he went on to write the music for BATS (1999), PITCH BLACK (2000), BELOW (2002), FREDDY VS. JASON (2003) and THE FOG (2005). Mary Ramos has a long career as music supervisor and music consultant. She has been the music supervisor in Quentin Taratino's films.

## DARK NIGHT
Written by: Dave Alvin
Performed by: The Blasters
Courtesy of Slash Records

This song is played over the opening credits. It will play a second time as the film closes and Kate leaves.

## AFTER DARK
Written by: Tito Larriva, Steven Huffsteder
Performed by: Tito & Tarantula

This is the song playing as Santanico Pandemonium (Salma Hayek) dances with the snake.

## ANGRY COCKROACHES
Written by: Tito Larriva, Peter Atanasoff
Performed by: Tito & Tarantula

This song plays as the characters enter the Titty Twister for the first time.

## TEXAS FUNERAL
Written by: David Vaught
Performed by: Jon Wayne

This song plays in the car as Richard waits for Seth to get a room at the motel.

## MARY HAD A LITTLE LAMB
Written by: Buddy Guy
Performed by: Stevie Ray Vaughan and Double Trouble
Courtesy of Epic Records
by arrangement with Sony Music Licensing

This song plays as the characters go sit at a table and start drinking.

WILLIE THE WIMP (AND HIS CADILLAC COFFIN)
Written by: Bill Carter and Ruth Ellen Ellsworth
Performed by Stevie Ray Vaughan and Double Trouble
Courtesy of Epic Records by arrangement with Sony Music
Licensing

This song plays as Seth and Richard shoot Razor Charlie and Richard gets bitten. The characters are attacked.

FOOLISH HEART
Written by: Raul Malo, Evan York
Performed by: The Mavericks
Courtesy of MCA Records

This song plays as Jacob, Kate and Scott are introduced.

DENGUE WOMAN BLUES
Written by: Jimmie Vaughan
Performed by: Jimmie Vaughan
Courtesy of Epic Records

This song plays as the characters travel inside the motorhome. Seth discovers that Jacob used to be an ordained minister.

JIMMIE'S JAM
Written by: Jimmie Vaughan
Performed by: Jimmie Vaughan
Courtesy of Epic Records

This song is played as the vampires attack.

## MEXICAN BLACKBIRD
Written by: Gibbons/Hill/Beard
Performed by: ZZ Top
Courtesy of Warner Brothers Records Inc.
by Arrangement with Warner Special Products

This song plays in the beginning of the film as the ranger enters the liquor store. It plays again as Jacob, Kate and Scott arrive at the motel and almost hit Seth.

## TORQUAY
Written by: George Tomsco
Performed by: The Leftovers

This song plays as the characters successfully cross the border into Mexico.

## OPENING BOXES
Written by Tito Larriva
Performed by Tito & Tarantula

This song is played as the surviving characters prepare do face the vampire horde.

## SHE'S JUST KILLING ME
Written by: Gibbons/Hill/Beard
Performed by: ZZ Top
Courtesy of BMG Music

This song plays as the characters arrive at the Titty Twister. It plays a second time over the end credits.

Original Motion Picture Soundtrack available on
LOS HOOLIGANS RECORDS/EPIC SOUNDTRAX

This record was released containing most of the licensed songs, snippets of dialogue from the film and some orchestral themes by Graeme Revell.

Stock Footage provided by
FILM & VIDEO STOCK SHOTS

The stock footage plays on the motel TV as Richard invites
their hostage to watch TV in bed with him.

## 14 – THE RETURN OF THE LIVING DEAD (1985)

With a soundtrack filled with 80's punk rock, THE RETURN OF THE LIVING DEAD is an example of a film whose soundtrack has become legendary. It was one of the first Hollywood films ever to rely on punk rock. The music credits are:

Music Composed by Matt Clifford
Music Producer for Film Trax Plc: Simon Heyworth
Music Consultant: Budd Carr
Music Assistants from Enigma: Steve Pross, William Hein
Additional Music: Robert Randles

Unlike most horror films, it advertises its music on the poster in order to boost its appeal to those who like the genre and direct people to the soundtrack.

The classical music we hear at Colonel Glover's house is in public domain. It is not credited in the film and came from a music library. Another song heard in the film, "PANZER ROLLEN IN AFRIKA VOR" is a Nazi song whose composer,

Norbert Schultze, handed to GEMA (a German collecting society) the control over his songs written between 1933 and 1945 and donated those royalties to the German Red Cross. Although not on the film's song list, it had to be cleared and paid for.

Main Title – "THE TRIOXIN THEME"
Performed by Francis Haines
Composed by Francis Haines
Produced by Simon Heyworth

This classic theme plays several times in the film, whenever we see the Trioxin at work. First during the main titles, second as the smoke from the crematorium mixes with rain and third in the aftermath of the atomic explosion. Variations of it can heard in other scenes as the crisis escalates.

"NOTHING FOR YOU"
Performed by T.S.O.L.
Composed by T.S.O.L.
Produced by Ron Goudie, Chris Gray and T.S.O.L.

This song plays as Freddy's friends are first seen walking on the sidewalk trying to figure out where to party.

"DEAD BEAT DANCE"
Performed by The Damned
Composed by The Damned
Produced by The Damned

This is played in the original film (1985) and HBO Video Release (VHS), but not in Hemdale's 1991 Release and subsequent versions. This is due to a rights issue. It had to be replaced by:

"YOUNG FAST IRANIANS"
Performed by Straw Dogs
Composed by Steve Grimes, Wayne Maestri
Produced by Steve Barry, and Straw Dogs

This song is the one we hear today in the film (since 1991), in the scene where Freddy's friends are driving.

"EYES WITHOUT A FACE"
Performed by The Flesheaters
Composed by Desjardins, Don Kirk, Robyn Jameson, Chris Wahl
Produced by Chris D.

This song plays as Freddy's friends enter the old Resurrection Cemetery.

"TONIGHT (WE'LL MAKE LOVE UNTIL WE DIE)"
Performed by SSQ
Composed by Jon St.James, Stacey Swain
Produced by Jon St.James for Formula One Music Productions

This song plays three times in the film. First, during the classic scene when Trash takes of her clothes and dances naked on top of a tomb. The song's title will be heard later by an isolated female voice as Trash returns as a zombie. The song will be played a third time during the end credits.

"PARTYTIME"
Performed by 45 Grave
Composed by Paul Cutler, Dinah Cancer, Don Bolles
Produced by Michael Wagener (of Double Trouble)

This song plays three times in the film. First on the aftermath of Trash's dance as she approaches Suicide. Later, it plays again as the zombies get out of their graves. It plays a third time at the end credits as it is implied that the Trioxin cycle will repeat itself and more zombies start to get out of their graves – starting a revue of the film's best moments. Although there are different versions of the song, the one that actually plays in the film is called "The Zombie Version". It is shorter and heavier than the previous versions.

### "LOVE UNDER WILL"
Performed by The Jet Black Berries
Composed by Gary Trainer
Produced by The Jet Black Berries

This song plays as Freddy's friends are in the cemetery and feel tired of waiting for him to show up. Tina decides to go to the warehouse and get him.

### "TAKE A WALK"
Performed by Tall Boys
Composed by Nigel Lewis, Mark Robertson
Produced by Mr. Fenstein

This song is played after Suicide is killed by Tar Man. His terrified friends run back into the cemetery, under the rain.

### "SURFIN' DEAD"
Performed by The Cramps
Composed by Ivy Rorschach, Lux Interior
Produced by The Cramps

This song is played as the characters barricade themselves inside the mortuary. The zombies are trying burst through the doors. It is also played a second time during the end credits.

### "BURN THE FLAMES"
Performed by Roky Erickson
Composed by Roky Erickson
Produced by Duane Aslaksen

This song is played as Frank cremates himself.

Original Soundtrack Album available on
Enigma
Records and Cassettes

Contrary to what happens with most films, THE RETURN OF
THE LIVING DEAD's soundtrack was entirely built around
one label's catalogue of artists. Having achieved such cult film
status, the soundtrack has been released in many formats.

## 15 – THE HUNGER (1983)

THE HUNGER is an interesting case study, since its title sequence and first scene features the English band Bauhaus onscreen lip-synching their classic song "BELA LUGOSI'S DEAD", written by David Haskins, Kevin Haskins, Peter Murphy and Daniel Ash. However, the song does not come credited in the end credits. Bauhaus comes credited among the cast as the band at the disco. The music credits are:

Original Music by Michel Rubini and Denny Jaeger
Music Supervised and Arranged by Howard Blake
Additional Electronic Music and Effects by David Lawson

The film contains a lot of classical music that is in public domain, especially arranged and conducted for the film by Howard Blake. It includes the duet "Viens, Malika... Dôme Épais le Jasmin" (AKA "The Flower Duet") from the opera "Lakmé" by Leo Delibes, two piano trios by Franz Schubert, the Violin Partita in E and a Cello Suite, by Johann Sebastian Bach, that the cast mimes in different scenes. One of those compositions, Schubert's Trio in E flat, was significantly altered to just contain the quieter parts. It is played during the film and through the end credits. Because all of those pieces are in public domain and are being newly arranged specifically for the film, the producers do not need to pay for a synchronization license. Because Howard Blake is using his own orchestra, new singers and making a new recording, there is also no need to pay for a master use. The film is creating its own master.

From these classical compositions, the only work that is not in public domain comes mentioned at the end credits:

"LE GIBET" by Maurice Ravel
Published by Arima and Durand SA

"Le Gibet" is part of the suite for piano "Garpard de la Nuit: Trois Poèmes pour Piano d'Après Aloysius Bertrand" by Maurice Ravel (1875-1937) that, at the time of the production, was not in public domain.

It is now. ☺

Another uncredited song used in the film is "FUNTIME" (written by David Bowie and Iggy Pop) sung by Iggy Pop, that plays as John attacks the skater. There are many reasons why a song plays uncredited in a film. Most times this happens because the song in question is public domain (without the need for paying for a synchronization license) and the production will be doing its own recording of it (without the need for a master use license). Clearly that's not the case here. Other reasons may apply: a musician who does not want to draw attention to his/her music and away from the film, contractual restrictions that forbid the inclusion of that artist (or his/her name) in projects not connected to his label, he/she is kindly giving it for free, etc.

## 16 – AN AMERICAN WEREWOLF IN LONDON (1981)

AN AMERICAN WEREWOLF IN LONDON is an interesting case study because its music soundtrack consists of songs that share a similar theme: the Moon. With that in mind, director John Landis went for high-profile songs that make the film quite memorable. Elmer Bernstein's compositions are very rich. However they are few as – contrary to most horror films – this film relies a lot on silence instead of music to create or amplify the mood.

Music by Elmer Bernstein
The Royal Philharmonic Orchestra
Conducted by Elmer Bernstein

Three versions of "BLUE MOON" mean clearing three different masters and paying for the same synch license three times.

"BLUE MOON"
Performed by Bobby Vinton
Courtesy of Columbia Records

This song is played during the main titles.

"BLUE MOON"
Performed by Sam Cooke
Courtesy of R.C.A. Records

This song can be heard during the classic transformation scene where David becomes a werewolf.

"MOONDANCE"
Performed by Van Morrison
Courtesy of Warner Bros. Records

This song plays as David and Alex make love in the shower. It's a heavily edited version of it that suits the film's editing.

"BAD MOON RISING"
Performed by Creedence Clearwater Revival
Courtesy of Fantasy Records

This song is heard as David stays alone in Alex's flat. As the night approaches, he becomes restless, impatient and puzzled for not being hungry.

"BLUE MOON"
Performed by The Marcels
Courtesy of Emus Records

This song is played at the end credits.

MECO'S IMPRESSIONS OF AN AMERICAN WEREWOLF
IN LONDON
Manufactured and Marketed by PolyGram Records

Interestingly enough, the film has very little orchestral music. With less than ten minutes of original music there was not enough to release an album. Meco, the American record producer and musician behind the disco version of the "STAR WARS THEME" (among other monstrosities) released this album, where he mixes sound-alike covers of the songs in the film (none of the masters used on the film can be found there) and includes some new material unrelated to the film.

## 17 – CASINO (1995)

Clocking at 178 minutes, Martin Scorsese's CASINO stands as the most fascinating and complex music soundtracks we know. It is also very long with a total of 62 songs. The film covers some 15 years in the life of Sam "Ace" Rothstein, who was given a casino to run by the Mafia. Being a period piece, the film relies heavily on music to recreate the period in question and accentuate an atmosphere of luxury, opulence, excess, crime and violence. The film has no original orchestral non-diegetic music, which makes this an interesting case of a film that skillfully communicates whatever the needs of the scene with pre-existing music only. That is possible because the whole story unfolds like party that, in the words of one of the characters: "but in the end, we fucked it all up". This means the whole story uses the glitzy casino sound ambience as a narrative style. One name appears over the first music credits card:

Music Consultant Robbie Robertson

Robbie Robertson has worked in the music department of several Scorsese films: THE KING OF COMEDY (1982), THE

COLOR OF MONEY (1986), CASINO, GANGS OF NEW YORK (2002), SHUTTER ISLAND (2010) and THE WOLF OF WALL STREET (2013). However, Robbie Robertson is also the lead guitarist and primary songwriter of famous Canadian-American rock group The Band, having written well-known songs like "The Weight" and "The Night They Drove Old Dixie Down". His collaboration with Scorsese dates back to THE LAST WALTZ (1978), a film that was produced by Robertson, and RAGING BULL (1980) to which Robertson contributed with songs.

A very interesting fact in this long music soundtrack is the predominance of big labels: MCA Records, EMI, Warner Bros. and Capitol Records. Many of the publishers are connected to those labels too, showing the concentration and the power of the big names when it comes to well-known songs and artists. That's unavoidable once you go for top names in terms of recognizability.

"J. S. Bach Matthauspassion BWV"
Performed by the Chicago Symphony Orchestra
Sir Georg Solti
Courtesy of the Decca Record Company Limited, London
by Arrangement with the PolyGram Film and TV Licensing

This piece makes an interesting choice to open the film for two reasons. First, because its somber nature gives the explosion of Ace's car, the title sequence and the monologue that sets the story context a depth and drama no other song could add. Second, because it draws a parallel between Jesus Christ and Ace Rothstein (who, although the audience don't know yet, will survive death and be reborn). The piece will return at the end as Ace reflects about Las Vegas today.

"Zooma Zooma"
Written by Paolo Citarella & Louis Prima
Performed by Louis Prima
Courtesy of Capitol Records
under License from CEMA Special Markets
Published by Shapiro, Bernstein & Co., Inc.

This song introduces the setting of the story: the Tangiers Casino in 1971 with Ace's introduction to himself as we see him arriving for just another night of work. This choice is relevant as it breaks completely with somber tone of Bach's classical piece. Louis Prima's loud vocal "O ma-mama, o ma-mama" and the blasting orchestra suggest the mood of an ongoing party. That confusion is Ace's normality and the audience lands right in the middle of it.

"Moonglow"/Love Theme From "Picnic"
Written by Eddie DeLange, Will Hudson,
Irving Mills/Morris Stoloff
Courtesy of MCA Records
Published by EMI Mills Music, Inc./
Scarsdale Music Corp.
Shapiro, Bernstein & Co., Inc. – Film Division

The choice of this song is surprising, since it is rare for a film to use songs from other films. However, being Scorsese a film buff himself, this choice is no surprise at all. The "counting room" sequence is famous for showing the secrecy and calmness inside those rooms. The man with the suitcase is "invisible" and his stealing doesn't affect those who see him come and go. This song helps set the idea that nothing of extraordinary is happening in that extraordinary place. It clearly breaks with the previous song as if shows the tranquility of the ever flowing money: "It's all been arranged just for us to get your money". The song, however, will be played again much later on the film as we go back to the counting room.

"You're Nobody 'Til Somebody Loves You"
Written by Russ Morgan & Larry Stock
Performed by Dean Martin
Courtesy of Capitol Records
under License from CEMA Special Markets
Published by Shapiro, Bernstein & Co., Inc./
Southern Music Publishing Co., Inc.

Dean Martin's voice sets the tone to the relaxed atmosphere you feel at the mobsters office in Kansas city. The soundtrack plays with the perception we all have of Dean Martin's suave persona and his connections to organized crime. It's exactly what we see: mobsters managing their millions in a very familiar scenario.

"Sing, Sing, Sing (With A Swing)"
Written and Performed by Louis Prima
Courtesy of Capitol Records
under License from CEMA Special Markets
Published by EMI Robbins Catalog Inc.

This song plays as the characters explain the wheels turning behind the birth of the Tangiers casino. The percussion adds some tension as the audience fully understand the risky connections between the casino and organized crime. It's a montage of moments that starts with Prima's scat singing. However, the song is edited as the montage advances so the more sinuous notes of the trumpet match the signature of frontman Philip Green. This song will return closer to the end as the FBI arrests everybody and closes the casino – confirming the tension created at the first time.

"7-11 (aka Mambo #5)"
Written by Perez Prado
Performed by The Gone All Stars
Courtesy of Rhino Records
by Arrangement with Warner Special Products
Published by Peer International Corporation

This song plays as Ace Rothstein walks the casino floor correcting the workers mistakes.

"Hoochie Koochie Man"
Written by Willie Dixon
Performed by Muddy Waters
Courtesy of MCA Records
Published by Hoochie Coochie Music
(Administered by Bug)

This song plays during the "Back Home Years Ago" sequence where we learn about Ace Rothstein origins as a guaranteed winner. The song will be featured a second time right after "(I Can't Get No) Satisfaction" by The Rolling Stones, when we see Ace observing the gamblers like a hawk.

"Fa-Fa-Fa-Fa-Fa (Sad Song)"
Written by Otis Redding & Steve Cropper
Performed by Otis Redding
Courtesy of Atco Records
by Arrangement with Warner Special Products
Published by Irving Music, Inc.

This song plays as Ace Rothstein delivers the winnings of his client, mob boss Remo Gaggi. This is one of those scenes where the song playing in the background is just background. But to Scorsese there is no background and even here we hear a great master.

"Long Long While"
Written by Mick Jagger & Keith Richards
Performed by The Rolling Stones
Published by ABKCO Music, Inc.
by Arrangement with ABKCO Records

This song plays during the scene where Nicky Santoro stabs a
man in a bar with a pen. This is the first song in the film by the
Rolling Stones. Scorsese is a Stones fan and uses their songs
many times in his films. The song will be cut after the stabbing
for Ace's monologue. A low, incomprehensible string of
echoes will carry the scene to it's conclusion.

"(I Can't Get No) Satisfaction"
Written by Mick Jagger & Keith Richards
Performed by The Rolling Stones
Published by ABKCO Music, Inc.
by Arrangement with ABKCO Records

After the stabbing and Ace's Monologue, the stabbing scene
resumes with a wide shot from the characters standing by the
empty bar. This song slowly emerges through the echoes that
show the shocked Ace. The song only lasts a few seconds
(mainly the song's refrain) before the next scene starts.

"The 'In' Crowd"
Written by Billy Page
Performed by Ramsey Lewis
Courtesy of MCA Records
Published by Unichappell Music, Inc.
& Elvis Presley Music
(All Rights Administered by Unichappell Music, Inc.)

This song starts right after the repetition of "Hoochie Koochie
Man" and marks the introduction of an incompetent employee
that Ace cannot fire because of his connections to a politician.
This event marks the monologue about the powerful politicians

whom the casino treats well. The chosen song could not be better: "The 'In' Crowd" talks about exactly that: a group of people who, for some reason, have everything. Here we hear the instrumental recorded live. This is just one of the many examples of moments where the scene borrows the essence of the song – showing the importance of choosing the right track. The song will continue through the story of Ishikawa, a Japanese millionaire who is lured back in the casino after winning two million.

"The 'In' Crowd"
Written by Billy Page
Performed by Dobie Gray
Courtesy of MCA Records
Published by Unichappell Music, Inc.
& Elvis Presley Music
(All Rights Administered by Unichappell Music, Inc.)

As the story funnels into how Ace manages to win over Ishikawa, the instrumental version transitions seamlessly into the classic vocal version by Dobie Gray. This is an example of how the instrumental version by Ramsey Lewis is used to introduce the theme that fully blooms into the full vocal version of the song, showing the triumph of the casino over Ishikawa. This transition is a masterpiece on how to combine songs for an accentuation of a story conclusion.

It's interesting to notice that part of the publishing of "The 'In' Crowd" is controlled by Elvis Presley Music. Elvis never recorded the song (as it was his practice to force writers to give him publishing rights over the songs he recorded), so it is possible that Billy Page's original publisher has been acquired and fused with Elvis Presley Music, since today, Warner/Chappell Music has control over 100% of the song.

"Compared To What"
Written by Eugene McDaniels
Performed by Les McCann & Eddie Harris
Courtesy of Atlantic Recording Corp.
by Arrangement with Warner Special Products
Published by Lonport Music Corp.

This song connects two moments: the ongoing monologue about the hierarchy of who watches who that leads to the introduction of Ginger. This is the first time we see her through the cameras – as Ace observes her.

The introduction of Ginger also brings the only moment in the film where there is true silence. As Ace observes her, we get the total absence of sound as a representation of the way she captures Ace's attention (beyond, of course, the characterization of that space a place of silence and observation).

The use of silence in CASINO only lasts a few seconds. However it is enough to cause a sense of strangeness in the audience, who is rarely treated by a film with true silence – especially in such an audio-rich film like this. However, the film is wise enough to not let the silence last until the audience starts to think there's a problem with the film. The sound returns as the camera goes back to the casino floor.

"Slippin' And Slidin'"
Written by Richard Penniman, Albert Collins
James Smith, Edwin Bocage
Performed by Little Richard
Courtesy of Specialty Records, Inc.
by Arrangement with Fantasy, Inc.
Published by ATV Music
Administered by EMI Blackwood Music, Inc.

As the camera moves back to the floor, we meet Ginger up

close, as she is accused of stealing chips from the rich man she's been with. The song will continue as Ginger gets angry and throws all his chips all up in the air as Ace – now on the floor – keeps observing her.

"Love Is Strange"
Written by Sylvia Robinson & Mickey Baker
Performed by Mickey and Sylvia
Courtesy of the RCA Record Label of BMG Music
Published by Ben-Ghazi Enterprises

A freeze frame in Ginger's smile to Ace sets the change into this song. The verse says it all "Baby, my sweet baby, you're the one". The instrumental ending of the song continues to play as Ginger walks in slow motion.

"Heart Of Stone"
Written by Mick Jagger & Keith Richards
Performed by The Rolling Stones
Published by ABKCO Music, Inc.
by Arrangement with ABKCO Records

Here is another song that seems to indicate the truth about a character, as Ace comments "for a girl like Ginger, love costs money". The song continues as we delve deeper into Ginger's world – as narrated by Ace.

"Love Is The Drug"
Written by Brian Ferry & Andrew Mackay
Performed by Roxy Music
Courtesy of Reprise Records
by Arrangement with Warner Special Products
and Courtesy of EG Records/Virgin Records Ltd.
Published by EG Music Ltd./BMG Music Publishing Ltd.
(Administered by BMG Music Publishing, Inc.)

This song plays as Ace explains the philosophy of Ginger as

she takes care of all the people in the casino. But the song also plays as we see her weakness: her pimp, Lester Diamond, here introduced of the first time.

"Nel Blu Dipinto Di Blu (Volare)"
Written by Domenico Modugno and Franco Migliacci
Performed by Domenico Modugno
Courtesy of Carosello Cemed S.R.L.
Published by Edizioni Curel, S.R.L. and
EMI Robbins Catalog Inc.

This song plays as we see Nicky Santoro smuggling diamonds.

"Takes Two To Tango"
Written by Al Hoffman & Dick Manning
Performed by Ray Charles & Betty Carter
Courtesy of Ray Charles Enterprises, Inc.
Published by All Hoffman Songs, Inc./
Dick Manning Music/Jewel Music Publishing Co., Inc.

This song plays as Nick Santoro and his wife meet Ginger in Vegas and get impressed by its opulence. The music continues through more scenes as Nick tells Ace he is moving into Vegas (thus the choice of "Takes Two To Tango" and the start of his operations in Vegas extorting money from people. This song fills several scenes about Nick's start in Vegas to which no specific mood is needed. Early on, we explained that Ray Charles created the exception by owning his own masters. You can see that by seeing "Ray Charles Enterprises" in the song credit.

"How High The Moon"
Written by Nancy Hamilton & Morgan Lewis
Performed by Les Paul & Mary Ford
Courtesy of Capitol Records
under License from CEMA Special Markets
Published by Chappell & Co.

This song plays as we move to another moment in Nick's life: working in the casino, scaring other criminals out of the casino.

"I Ain't Superstitious"
Written by Willie Dixon
Performed by Jeff Beck
Courtesy of Epic Records
by Arrangement with Sony Music Licensing
Published by Hoochie Coochie Music
(Administered by Bug)

This is one fascinating use for Jeff Back's 1968 version of Willie Dixon's classic (with Rod Stewart on the vocals, no less). The guitar's cries along with the drumming breaks create a breathtaking tension as Ace narrates the cheater's scheme and executes his plan of attack. This is the second Willie Dixon song to appear on the film. Concentrating some of the licensing to the same labels or publishers make the producer's life easier – especially when dealing with so many songs.

"Happy Birthday To You"
Written by Patty and Mildred Hill
Published by Summy-Birchard Music

This song is sung by female waiters through the previous song as a decoy created by the casino to attract attention away from the imminent attack on the cheaters.

The scene where the cheater gets his hand smashed with a hammer has no music. That choice (again, silence) characterizes that room as an inaccessible place, far from the happy casino mood. It's also confirmed by Ace's narration when he says: "we had to make an example of these pricks that the party was over".

"Working In The Coal Mine"
Written by Allen Toussaint
Performed by Lee Dorsey
Courtesy of Arista Records
Published by Screen Gems – EMI Music Inc.

The use of this song as the second cheater tries to quietly leave
with the Money and is lured in by Don Rickles' character
shows how carefully CASINO uses music – in this case with
extreme sense of humor. The song will be played a second time
later after the Ace fires the incompetent slots manager.

"Unforgettable"
Written by Irving Gordon
Performed by Dinah Washington
Courtesy of Verve Records
by Arrangement with Polygram Film and TV Licensing
Published by Bourne Co.

This song sets a different tone, as Ace asks Ginger in marriage.
The scene is long and the music helps set the mood for what
Ace is trying to achieve (and his ultimate ingenuity).

"Stardust" (Instrumental)
Written by Hoagy Carmichael
Courtesy of The RCA Records Label of BMG Music
Published by EMI Mills Music Inc. /
Hoagy Publishing Company

This scene plays as Ace and Ginger get married.

"Stardust" (Vocal)
Written by Hoagy Carmichael
Courtesy of The RCA Records Label of BMG Music
Published by EMI Mills Music Inc. /
Hoagy Publishing Company

This vocal version of the song plays after the phone call between Ginger and Lester. Here, again, the film morphs an instrumental version into a vocal version as we get closer to the characters. This version will play again later, as the Remo Gaggi asks Frank about Nicky and Ginger.

"What A Difference A Day Makes"
Written by Stanley Adams & Maria Grever
Performed by Dinah Washington
Courtesy of Verve Records
by Arrangement with PolyGram Film & TV Licensing
Published by Zomba Golden Sands Enterprises, Inc./
Edward B. Marks Music Co. on behalf of itself
& Stanley Adams Music

This is a well-known master that plays as we see Ginger's new married life. The sheer lush and sophistication of the song brings all its qualities into the scene.

"I'll Take You There"
Written by Alvertis Isbell
Performed by The Staple Singers
Courtesy of Fantasy, Inc.
Published by Irving Music, Inc.

This song plays as Ace puts money in the bank on Ginger's name. Again, a well-chosen title.

"Love Me The Way I Love You"
Written by Charles Tobias
Performed by Jerry Vale
Courtesy of The Robert Vale Record Co.
Published by Ched Music Corp. and Ritvale Music Corp.

Jerry Vale lipsynchs his own song. The film credits him as "archive footage", but that's very unlikely to be the image of him we see on the film. It is possible that the producers cleared the footage, but managed to get him anyway. Jerry also appeared in Scorsese's GOODFELLAS (1990)

"Let's Start All Over Again"
Written by Elsa Byrd & Paul Winley
Performed by The Paragons
Courtesy of Collectable Records
Published by Ninny Publishing Co.

This song plays as we see Nicky's business bringing danger to Ace. Their relationship starts to get stressed.

"Sweet Virginia"
Written by Mick Jagger & Keith Richards
Performed by The Rolling Stones
Courtesy of Promotone B.V.
Published by ABKCO Music, Inc.

This song (another Rolling Stones classic) plays as the casino security throws out one of Nicky's men for putting his feet on the table. It keeps playing as the Nicky and Ace talk about it over the telephone and Nicky beats his employee for disrespecting Ace.

"Basin Street Blues/When It's Sleepy Time Down South"
Written by Spencer Williams/Clarence Muse,
Leon Rene, Otis Rene
Performed by Louis Prima
Courtesy of Capitol Records
under License from CEMA Special Markets
Published by Edwin H. Morris & Company, a division of
MPL Communications, Inc./EMI Mills Music Inc. and
Screen Gems – EMI Music Inc.

This song plays as Ace sets his standard of quality for the casino entertainment and brings his own innovations. But the interesting thing about this master is that you getting two different songs in the same master: "Basin Street Blues" (Spencer Williams) and "When It's Sleepy Time Down South" (Muse/René/René). Louis Prima makes both songs sound like two different masters (the rhythm of the songs is different, for example) and the film uses them in a sequence. The second part continues as Nicky beats up people on the street and Ace tries to warn him that he is going too far.

"Stella By Starlight"
Written by Ned Washington & Victor Young
Performed by Ray Charles
Courtesy of Ray Charles Enterprises, Inc.
Published by Famous Music Corporation

This song plays as Ace gets an award while Ginger seems to glow as his wife. That's the second master by Ray Charles licensed by the film and it appears again a few minutes later for a few seconds (right after the next song) as Ginger eats with friends. By concentrating at least part of the licensing between certain labels and publishers, the producers may negotiate better terms.

"Boogaloo Down Broadway"
Written by Jesse James
Performed by The Fantastic Johnny C.
Courtesy of Phil – L.A. of Soul Records
Published by Dandelion Music

Another example of the film's sense of humor as Ace scolds an incompetent (yet unfirable) slots manager.

"Sweet Dreams"
Written by Don Gibson
Performed by Emmylou Harris
Courtesy of Reprise Records
by Arrangement with Warner Special Products
Published by Acuff-Rose Music, Inc.

This song plays as we learn Nicky gets banned from Las Vegas. The choice of this master is interesting because the song is more associated with Patsy Cline who had a big hit with it in 1963. However, this master is less lush and probably cheaper. Scorsese used the song again in his film THE DEPARTED (2006).

"Can't You Hear Me Knocking"
Written by Mick Jagger & Keith Richards
Performed by The Rolling Stones
Courtesy of Promotone B.V.
Published by ABKCO Music, Inc.

Another classic by The Rolling Stones and the second master the film licensed from Promotone B.V. (the company who owns the band's masters, set by the band themselves in the Netherlands for tax reasons. All the publishing is controlled in America by ABKCO. This song plays as Nicky Santoro hires his own gang to terrorize Vegas. The song plays for several minutes during the montage as the group commits all kinds of crimes and expands business.

"Toad"
Written by Peter Edward Baker
Performed by Cream
by Arrangement with PolyGram Film & TV Licensing
Published by Chappell & Co. o/b/o Dratleaf Ldt.

Cream's first song on the film plays as Nicky recounts a massacre that that happened at Remo Gaggi's bar and the subsequent torture that took place (the "head on the vice" scene). The song is played edited and will be played a second time later during a recorded phone call between Ace and Nicky, a third time (solo drumming) as Ace waits for Nicky in the desert, and a fourth time as Ace prepares to meet Ginger in the morning.

"Those Were The Days"
Written by Ginger Baker and Peter Constantine Brown
Performed by Cream
Courtesy of PolyGram International Music BV
by Arrangement with PolyGram Film & TV Licensing
Published by Chappell & Co. o/b/o Dratleaf Ltd.

The second Cream song comes in sequence as Ace scolds the incompetent slots manager again and fires him.

"Hurt"
Written by Jimmie Crane & Al Jacobs
Courtesy of EMI Records
under License from CEMA Special Markets
Published by EMI Miller Catalog Inc.

This song plays as Ginger asks Ace for money. This song signals the beginning of the end of Ace's happiness.

"The Glory Of Love"
Written by Billy Hill
Performed by The Velvetones
Courtesy of EMI Records
under License from CEMA Special Markets
Published by Shapiro, Bernstein & Co., Inc.

This song plays as Ginger takes money from the bank for Lester Diamond. The song plays again a few seconds later as Ace confronts Ginger and Lester. It will play a third time later as the FBI photographs Ginger's affair with Nicky.

"Nights In White Satin"
Written by Justin Hayward
Performed by The Moody Blues
Courtesy of Threshold/Polydor/Atlas Records
by Arrangement with PolyGram Film & TV Licensing
Published by TRO-Essex Music, Inc.

This song plays as Ginger complains to Nicky about Ace.

"Walk On The Wild Side"
Written by Elmer Bernstein & Mack David
From the Columbia Film "Walk On The Wild Side"
Performed by Jimmy Smith
Courtesy of Verve Records
by Arrangement with PolyGram Film & TV Licensing
Published by Shapiro, Bernstein & Co., Inc. –
Film Division

This song plays as the mob bosses discuss the fact that people are stealing their money. This is one more master the film licenses from Verve Records. The song plays through several scenes and culminates with the murder of Anna Scott.

"Gimme Shelter" (Live Version)
Written by Mick Jagger & Keith Richards
Performed by The Rolling Stones
Courtesy of Promotone B.V.
Published by ABKCO Music, Inc.

Another classic from The Rolling Stones. This one plays as the Nicky gets blamed for all the murders happening in Vegas. This is a live version and not the original master. It will play a second time as Nicky beats someone and feels tired.

"Gimme Shelter"
Written by Mick Jagger & Keith Richards
Performed by The Rolling Stones
Published by ABKCO Music, Inc.
by Arrangement with ABKCO Records

This classic master appears together with the live version. Both are edited together. The mixing of live versions and classic masters happens many times in films because of the cost of using classic masters over several scenes or long passages.

"EEE-O Eleven"
Written by Sammy Cahn and Jimmy Van Heusen
Performed by Sammy Davis Jr.
Published by Maraville Music Corp.

This song plays during the sequence where Nicky and Ace complain about their problems.

"I'll Walk Alone"
Written by Jule Styne and Sammy Cahn
Performed by Don Cornell
Courtesy of MCA Records
Published by WB Music Corp. o/b/o Cahn Music Co.

This song plays as Piscano at his grocery store complains about the lack of suitcases while the FBI hears is all.

"Sunrise" (Prelude From "2001: A Space Odyssey")
Composed by Richard Strauss
Performed by The Chicago Symphony Orchestra
Courtesy of RCA Victor Red Seal
A Division of BMG Classics

This song plays briefly as the opening of Ace's TV show ACES HIGH.

"That's The Way I Like It"
Written by Harry Wayne Casey
Published by Windswept Pacific Entertainment Co.
dba Longitude Music Co.

This classic disco song immortalized by K.C. & the Sunshine Band plays in the continuation of the Ace's TV show. This master, however, is not the original, but a cheaper version that emulates a bad TV show.

Flight Of The Bumblebee
Performed by Jascha Heifetz
Courtesy of RCA Victor Red Seal
A Division of BMG Classics

Another song from the TV show as Ace Juggles as a violinist plays.

"Venus"
Written by Edward H. Marshall
Published by ATV Music administered by
EMI April Music Inc. and Welbeck Music Corp.

A cheap sounding version of this song immortalized by Frankie Avalon plays as the artist is featured as a guest on Ace's TV show.

"Theme De Camille"
From the Motion Picture "Le Mepris"
Composed by Georges Delarue
Courtesy of Sidomusic/B. Liechtl & Co.

This song plays as Ace waits for Nicky on the desert. On top of it, there is a excerpt of the drumming solo from Cream's "Toad". The song will play a second time as Ace and Ginger drive home after she returns. It will play a third time as Ace discovers Ginger on the phone talking about killing him. It will play a fourth time as Ace throws Ginger out. It will return a fifth time as Ace closes the story and the final credits start.

"Whip It"
Written by Mark Motherabaugh & Gerald Casale
Performed by Devo
Courtesy of Warner Bros. Records Inc.
by Arrangement with Warner Special Products
and Courtesy of Virgin Records Ltd.
Published by EMI Virgin Songs, Inc.

This song plays on the scene where Ace pretends not to know Nicky at the casino as Ace dines with friends. This is the first song by DEVO that plays on the film.

"Ain't Got No Home"
Written and Performed by Clarence Henry
Courtesy of MCA Records
Published by Arc Music Corporation

This song plays as Nicky abuses the casino dealer and Ace tries to make him leave.

"I'm Sorry"
Written by Ronnie Self and Dub Albritten
Performed by Brenda Lee
Courtesy of MCA Records
Published by Champion Music Corporation

This song plays as Ace thinks about his marriage and learns Ginger is back with Lester Diamond.

"Without You"
Written by Pete Ham and Tom Evans
Performed by Harry Nilsson
Courtesy of the RCA Records Label of BMG Music
Published by WB Music Corp. o/b/o Apple Publishing

This classic song plays as Lester Diamond tries to flee with Ginger. And she calls Nicky.

"Go Your Own Way"
Written by Lindsay Buckingham
Performed by Fleetwood Mac
Courtesy of Warner Bros. Records Inc.
by Arrangement with Warner Special Products
Published by Now Sounds Music

This song plays as Ace and Andy talk in the car so no one can listen to them.

"I'm Confessin' (That I Love You)"
Performed by Louis Prima & Keely Smith
Written by Doc Dougherty, Al Neiburg, Ellis Reynolds
Courtesy of MCA Records
Published by Bourne Co.

This song plays as Ace and Ginger have dinner and he confronts her with the money she spent with Lester. This is the fourth song sung by Louis Prima.

"The Thrill Is Gone"
Written by Roy Hawkins & Rick Darnell
Performed by B. B. King
Courtesy of MCA Records
Published by Powerforce/Careers –
BMG Music Publishing, Inc.
(Administered by Careers – BMG Music Publishing, Inc.)

This classic song plays as Ginger talks to Nicky and the two start an affair.

"(I Can't Get No) Satisfaction"
Performed by Devo
Courtesy of Warner Bros. Inc.
by arrangement with Warner Special Products
and Courtesy of Promotone B.V.
Published by ABKCO Music Inc.

This song plays as a war starts between the police and Nicky's men. It will play a second time as Ace goes home to discover his daughter tied to the bed. It will play a third time as Ace calls Billy Sherbert asking for a gun. It plays a fourth time as Billy arrives with the gun.

"Who Can I turn To (When Nobody Needs Me)"
Written by Leslie Bricusse & Anthony Newley
Performed by Tony Bennett
Courtesy of Columbia Records
by Arrangement with Sony Music Licensing
Published by TRO-Essex Music, Inc.

This song plays as Ace confronts Ginger at Nicky's restaurant.

"Harbor Lights"
Written by Jimmy Kennedy and Hugh Williams
Performed by The Platters
Courtesy of Mercury Records
by Arrangement with PolyGram Film & TV Licensing
Published by Chappell & Co. o/b/o Peter Maurice Music

This song plays as Ginger goes back to Nicky's restaurant and gets thrown out by him. There are several masters of this song. This one by The Platters is not one of the most well-known.

"The House Of The Rising Sun"
Written by Allan Price
Performed by The Animals
by Arrangement with ABKCO Records
and EMI Records Ltd.
Published by EMI Al Gallico Music Corp.

This song plays as Ace sees the photos of Nicky and Ginger and the mobsters go to trial and Remo Gaggi decides it's safer to kill everybody who can talk. The song will continue as the men get killed. It gets reverb added when it shows Ginger's death. It returns for Ace's near death experience and Nicky Santoro's violent death.

Let's go over the numbers regarding masters:
- 9 Masters from MCA.
- 9 Masters from PolyGram.
- 7 Masters from Warner.
- 6 Masters from RCA.
- 6 Masters from CEMA.
- 5 Masters from ABKCO.
- 4 Masters from Promotone B.V.
- 2 Masters from Sony Music.
- 2 Masters from Reprise.
- 2 Masters from Ray Charles Enterprises.
- The number of publishers is more diluted, but still we can find some repetitions:
- 12 times: EMI.
- 8 times: ABKCO Music.
- 6 times: Warner/Chappell Music.
- 4 times: Shapiro, Bernstein & Co.

The CASINO music soundtrack seems to match most of the possibilities we discussed on chapter one regarding music: it helps set the time when the action takes place, it sets mood and ambience, it reinforces character's psychology, it synchronizes characters and audience, it distends time (or compresses it), it enhances emotions, it helps create empathy, it brings recognizability to the score, it helps marketing and it is fun. These are just some of the reasons why this soundtrack is so important.

This is the soundtrack that was released on CD when the film came out:
- Contempt - Theme De Camille - Georges Delerue (Sidomusic/B. Liechtl & Co.)
- Angelina/Zooma, Zooma Medley - Louis Prima (CEMA)
- Hoochie Coochie Man - Muddy Waters (MCA)
- I'll Take You There – The Staple Singers (Fantasy)
- Nights In White Satin - The Moody Blues (PolyGram)
- How High The Moon - Les Paul & Mary Ford (CEMA)
- Hurt - Timi Yuro (CEMA)
- Ain't Got No Home - Clarence 'Frogman' Henry (MCA)
- Without You – Nilsson (RCA)
- Love Is The Drug - Roxy Music (Warner)
- I'm Sorry - Brenda Lee (MCA)
- Go Your Own Way - Fleetwood Mac (Warner)
- The Thrill Is Gone - B.B. King (MCA)
- Love Is Strange - Mickey And Sylvia (RCA)
- The 'In' Crowd - Ramsey Lewis (MCA)
- Walk On The Wild Side - Jimmy Smith (PolyGram)
- Fa-Fa-Fa-Fa-Fa (Sad Song) - Otis Redding (Warner)
- I Ain't Superstitious - Jeff Beck With Rod Stewart (Sony)
- The Glory Of Love - The Velvetones (CEMA)
- (I Can't Get No) Satisfaction – Devo (Warner)
- What A Difference A Day Makes - Dinah Washington (PolyGram)
- Working In A Coal Mine - Lee Dorsey (Arista)
- House Of The Rising Sun - Eric Burdon (NOT THE MASTER IN THE FILM)
- Those Were The Days – Cream (PolyGram)
- Who Can I Turn To (When Nobody Needs Me) - Tony Bennett (Sony)

- Slippin' And Slidin' - Little Richard (Fantasy)
- You're Nobody Till Somebody Loves You - Dean Martin (CEMA)
- Compared To What - Les McCann & Eddie Harris (Warner)
- Basin Street Blues/ When It's Sleepy Time Down South - Louis Prima (CEMA)
- Matthaus Passion - Chicago Symphony Orchestra (PolyGram)

Here are some interesting things about this soundtrack:
- The bigger labels are overwhelmingly represented (the soundtrack itself released by MCA – at the time, sister company of Universal Pictures, the film's distributor).
- The replacement of one of the masters, "House of the Rising Sun", by a newer one sung by Eric Burdon (the same vocalist, but without The Animals) – similar to the situation we described in the question "But the master is so protected and expensive. What can I do?"
- There are some notable omissions, like "Moonglow/Love Theme from Picnic" that plays during one of the film's most memorable scenes, the Ray Charles' songs or any of the several masters by The Rolling Stones (we only get Devo's version of one). Sometimes these masters are too expensive, other times the owner just does not want to let them out.

However, the songs that remain are still an impressive list of great songs and masters that represent more than well the film. Also of notice is the fact that the album is produced by Robbie Robertson with Scorsese, Barbara De Fina and Thelma Schoonmaker as executive producers. You can hardly ask for more.

## 18 – FINAL NOTES

By now, you must have realized the seriousness of licensing music for films. However, like in anything, practice makes perfect. After one or two films, you'll automatically know your way around the issue. Feel free to share this guide with people you know and remember to watch and support horror films.

NOW A BIG DISCLAIMER:
THIS BOOK DOES NOT CONSTITUTE LEGAL ADVICE. WE ARE NOT LAWYERS. YOU SHOULD ALWAYS, ALWAYS, ALWAYS HAVE A LAWYER TO HELP YOU WITH LEGAL STUFF. IN FACT, WE ARE JUST A GROUP OF HORROR GEEKS WHO LOVE HORROR FILMS AND FEEL LIKE HELPING OTHER FILMMAKERS LIKE US WITH ISSUES WE FACE IN FILMMAKING. SO, THE INFORMATION, COMMENTS AND OPINIONS PROVIDED HERE ARE JUST THE RESULT OF OUR EXPERIENCE, STUDY AND PAST MISTAKES. HOWEVER (AGAIN) TO THE DISAPPOINTMENT OF OUR MOTHERS WE ARE NOT LAWYERS SO ALWAYS CONSULT WITH THE PEOPLE WHO KNOW: YOU GUESSED IT: LAWYERS! THEY WOULD AGREE WITH US.

If you enjoyed this book, please leave a review.
Also, the author will be publishing "FILM MARKETING FOR
INDEPENDENT AND LOW BUDGET FILMS" soon.